11+ Non-verbal Reasoning

WORKBOOK 4

Additional Practice Questions

Dr Stephen C Curran
with Andrea Richardson
Edited by Katrina MacKay

This book belongs to

Accelerated Education Publications Ltd

© 2011 Stephen Curran

Contents

17. Odd One Out   Pages

1. Basic Level   4-7
2. Intermediate Level   8-11
3. Advanced Level   12-15
4. Higher Level   16-19
5. Mixed Levels   20-23

18. Codes

1. Type 1 - Level Two   24-27
2. Type 2 - Level Two   28-31
3. Type 1 - Level Three   32-35
4. Type 1 - Level Four   36-39
5. Mixed Levels   40-43

19. Analogies

1. Level One   44-47
2. Level Two   48-51
3. Level Three   52-55
4. Levels Four & Five   56-59
5. Mixed Levels   60-63

© 2011 Stephen Curran

Chapter Seventeen
ODD ONE OUT
1. Basic Level

In each of the rows below there are five figures. Find one figure in each row that is **most unlike** the other four.

Example

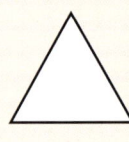 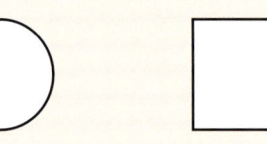 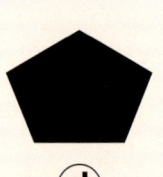 

a   b   c   ⓓ   e

Answer: **d** as it is the only Black shape.

Exercise 17: 1 Which figure does not fit in with the others?

1)

   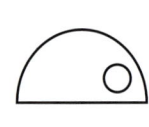 

a   b   c   d   e

2)

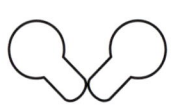 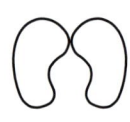  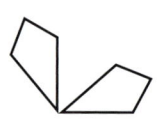 

a   b   c   d   e

3)

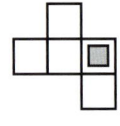 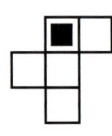 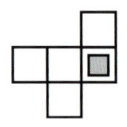 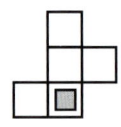 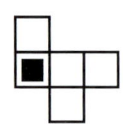

a   b   c   d   e

4)

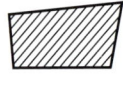  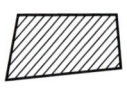 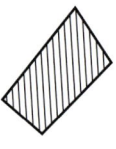 

a   b   c   d   e

© 2011 Stephen Curran

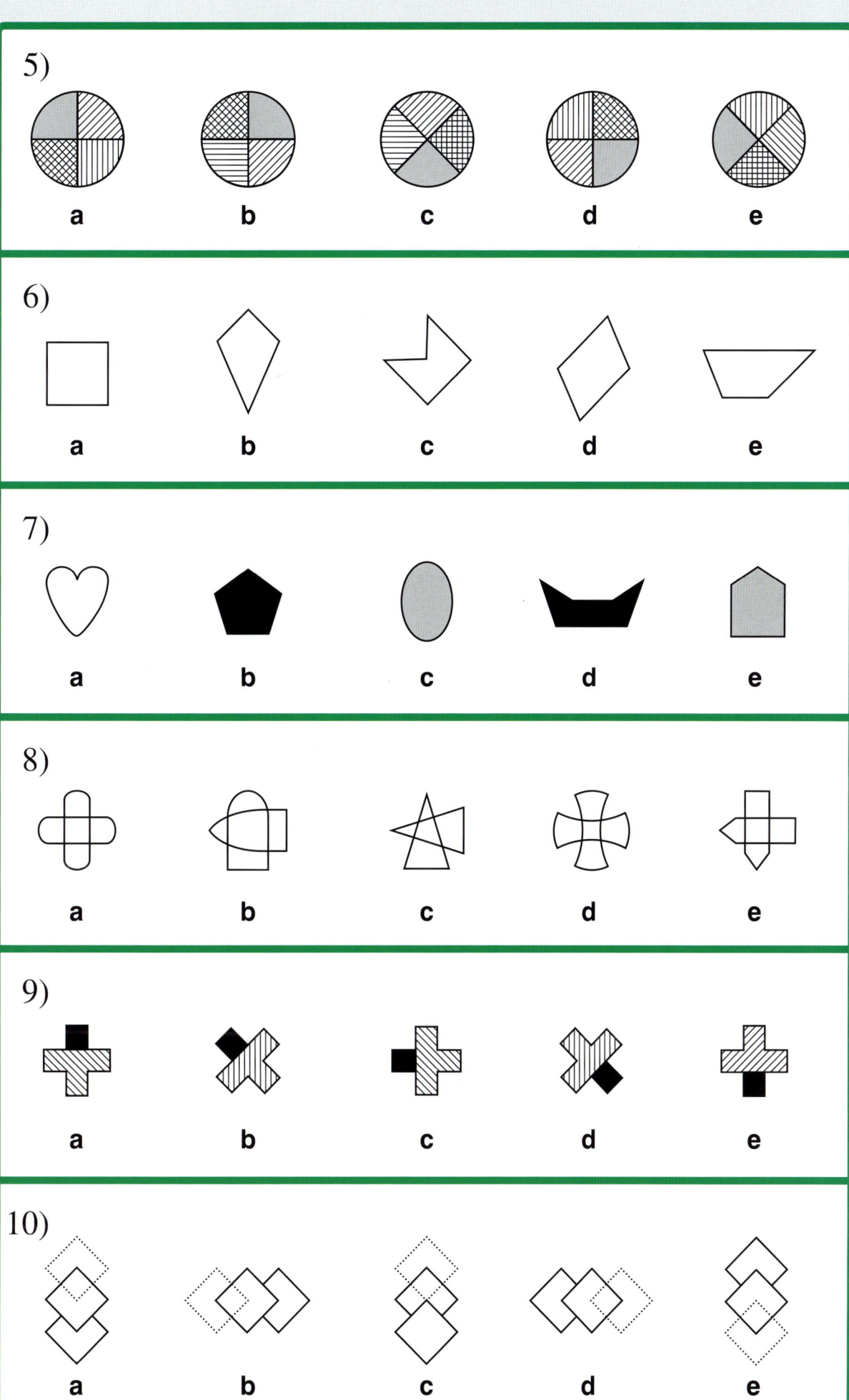

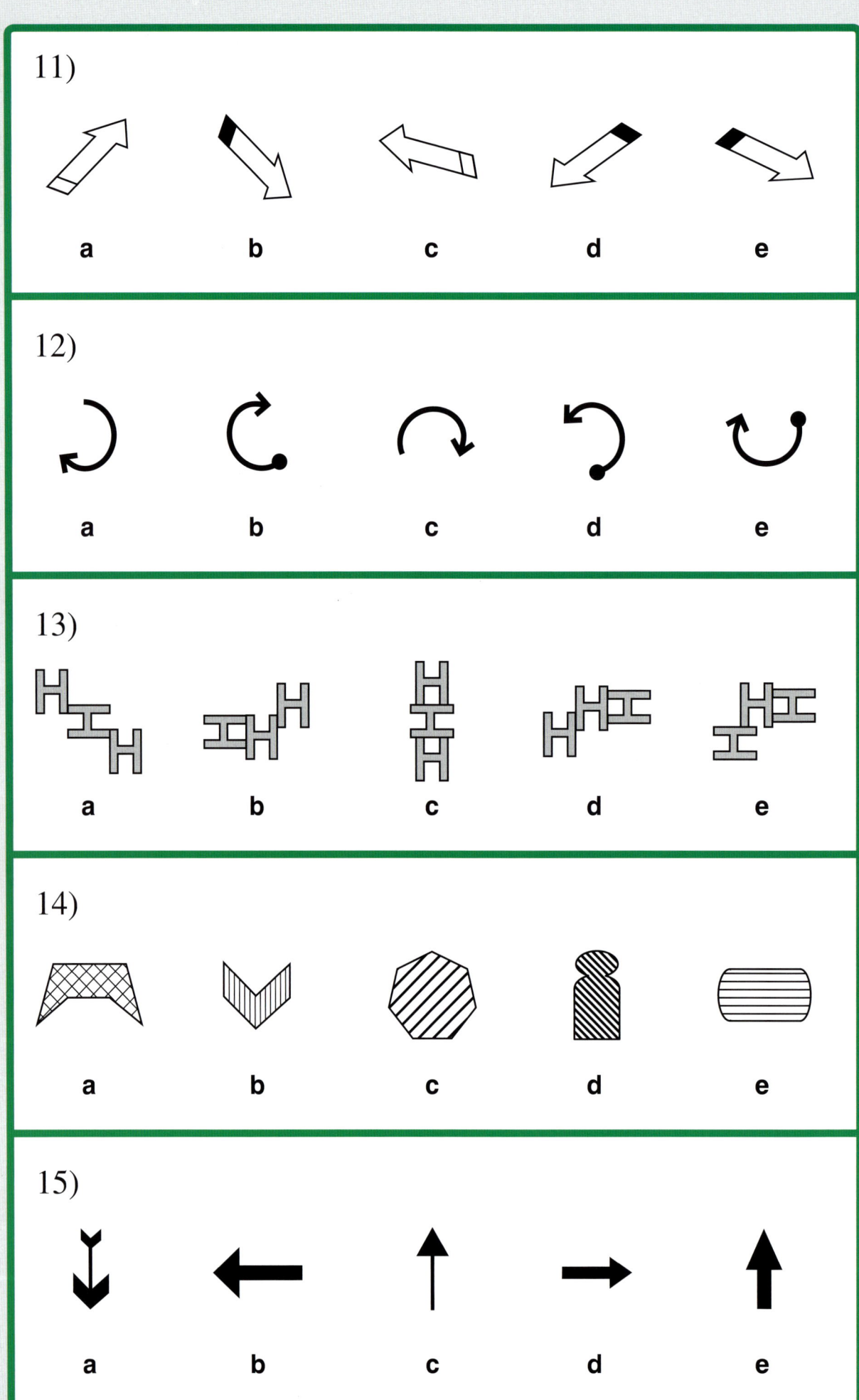

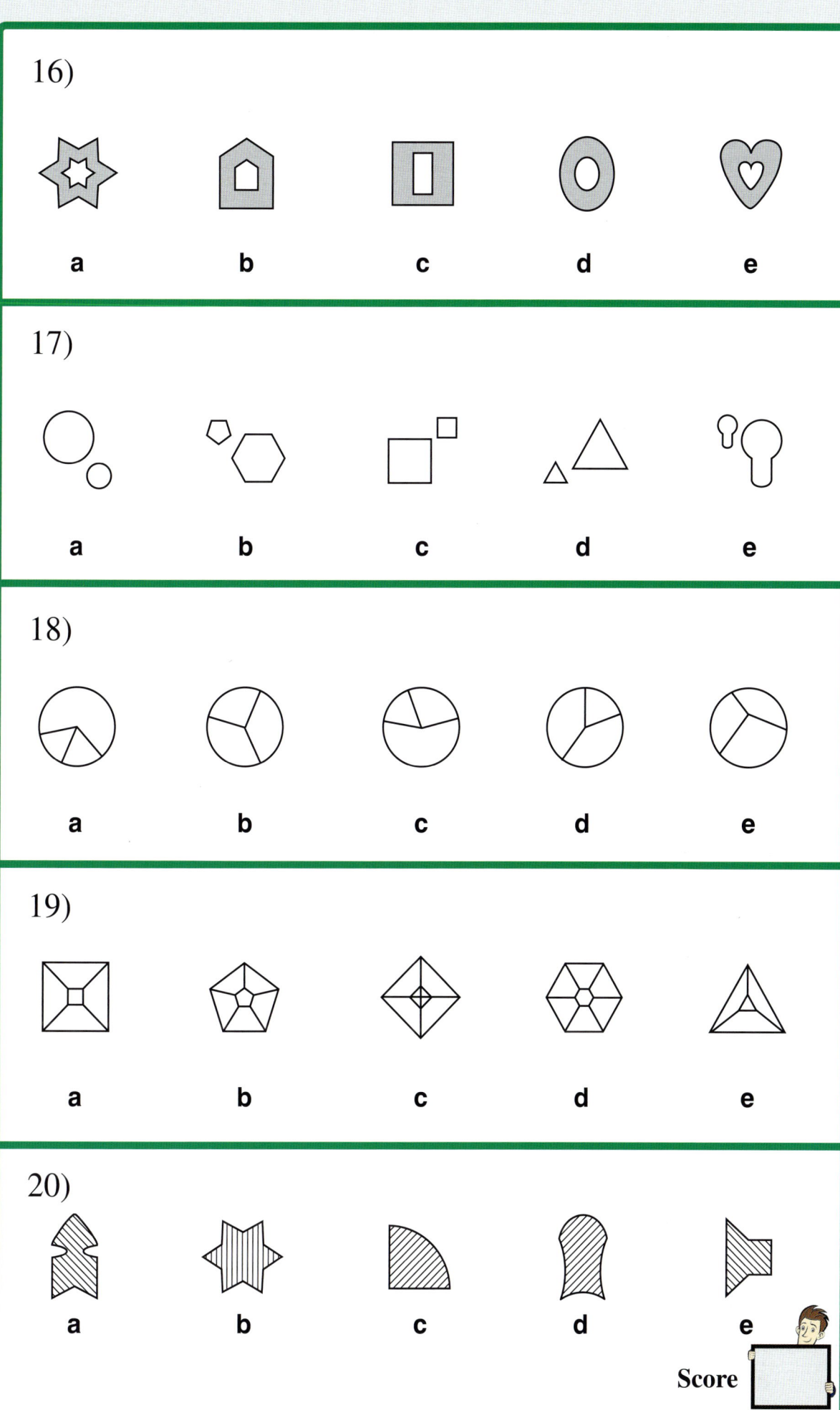

2. Intermediate Level

In each of the rows below there are five figures. Find one figure in each row that is **most unlike** the other four.

Example

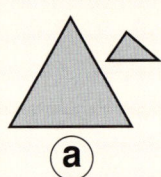  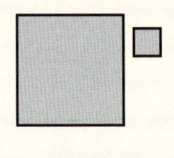  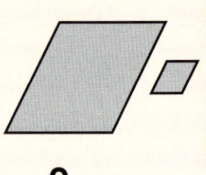

a   b   c   d   e

Answer: **a** as the smaller shape is not the same as the larger shape.

Exercise 17: 2 Which figure does not fit in with the others?

1)

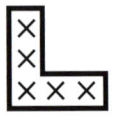   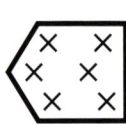 

a   b   c   d   e

2)

  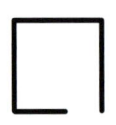  

a   b   c   d   e

3)

  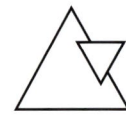 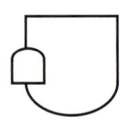 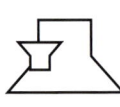

a   b   c   d   e

4)

 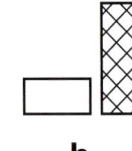 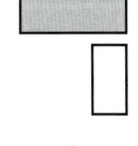  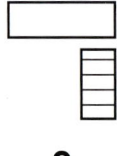

a   b   c   d   e

© 2011 Stephen Curran

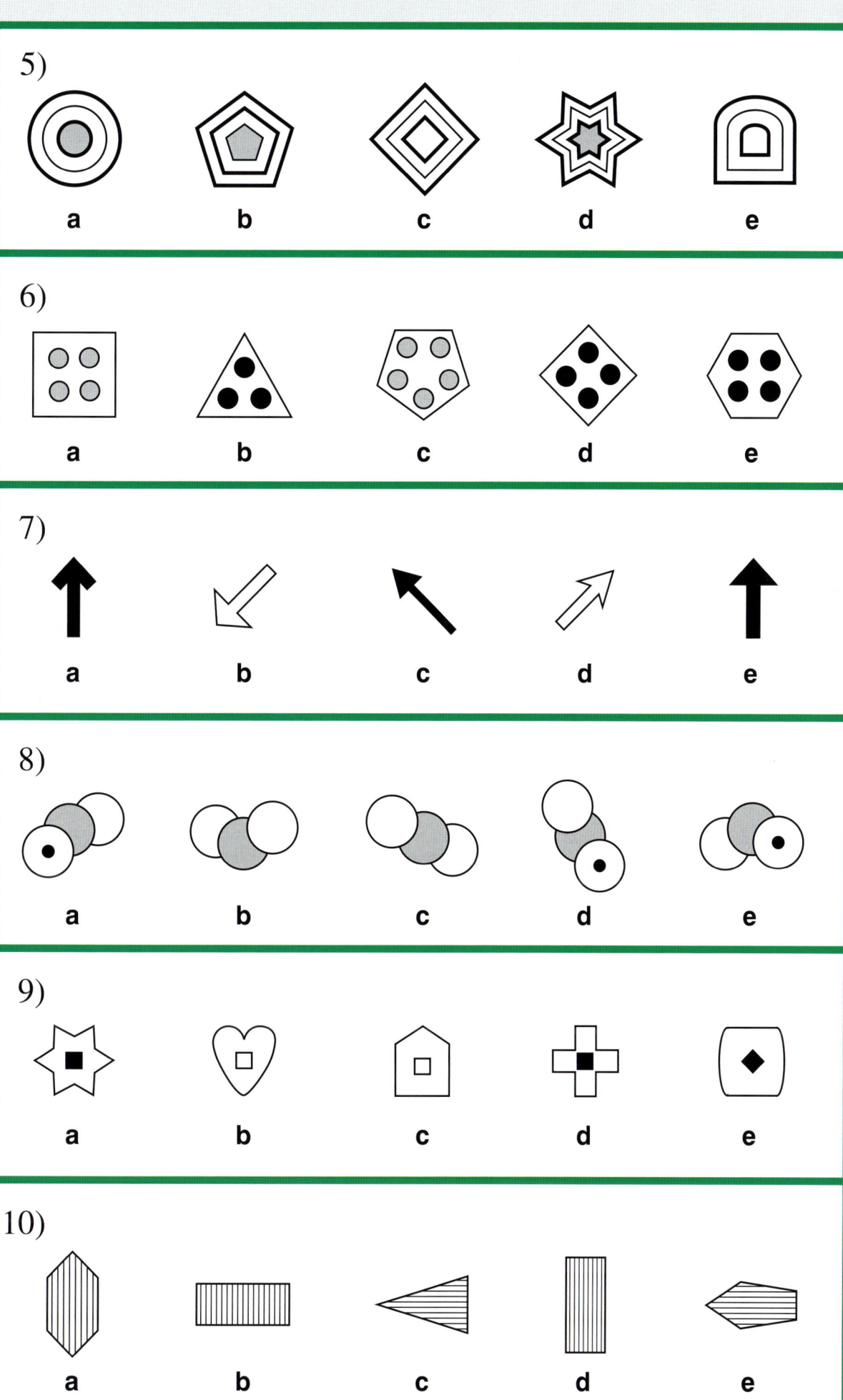

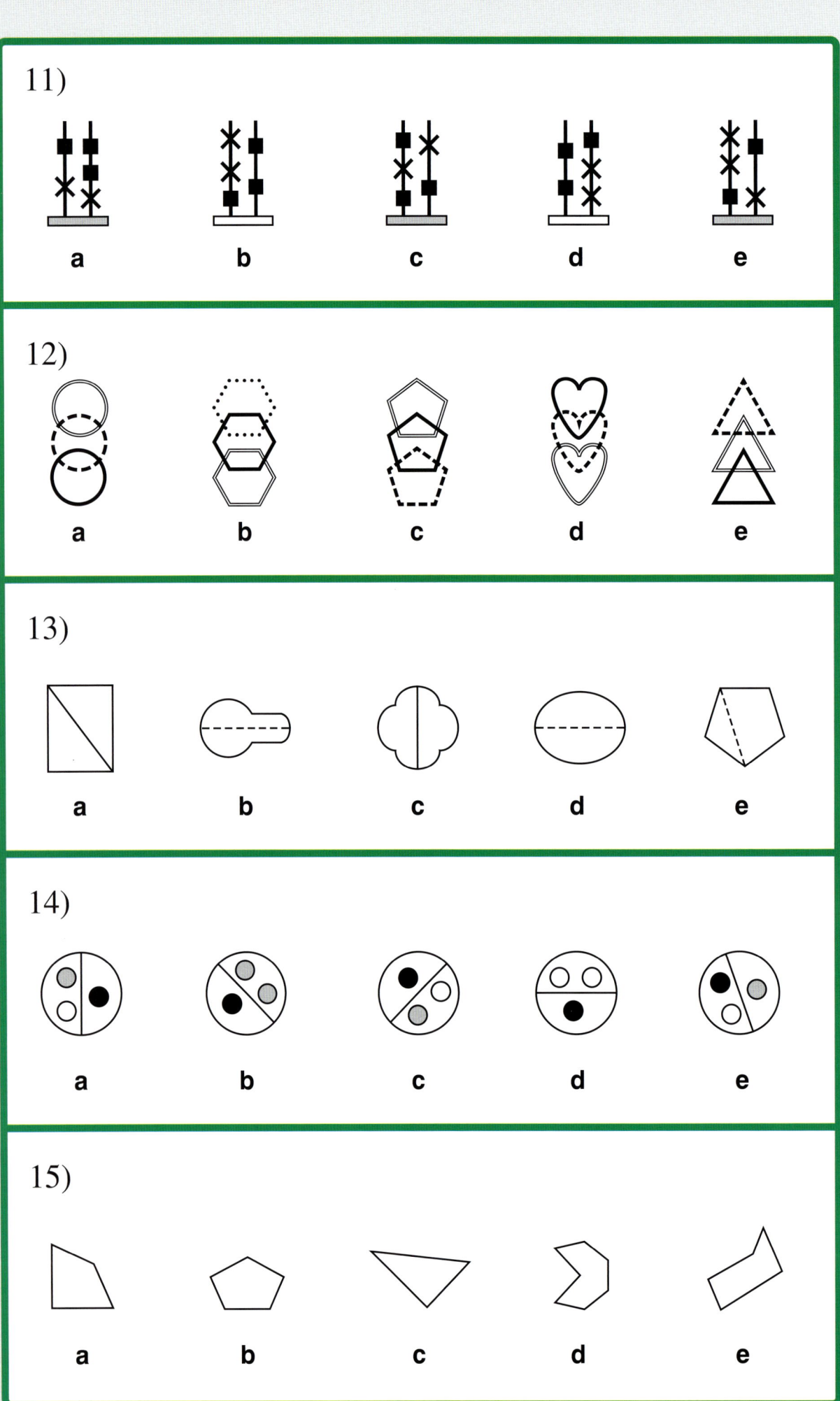

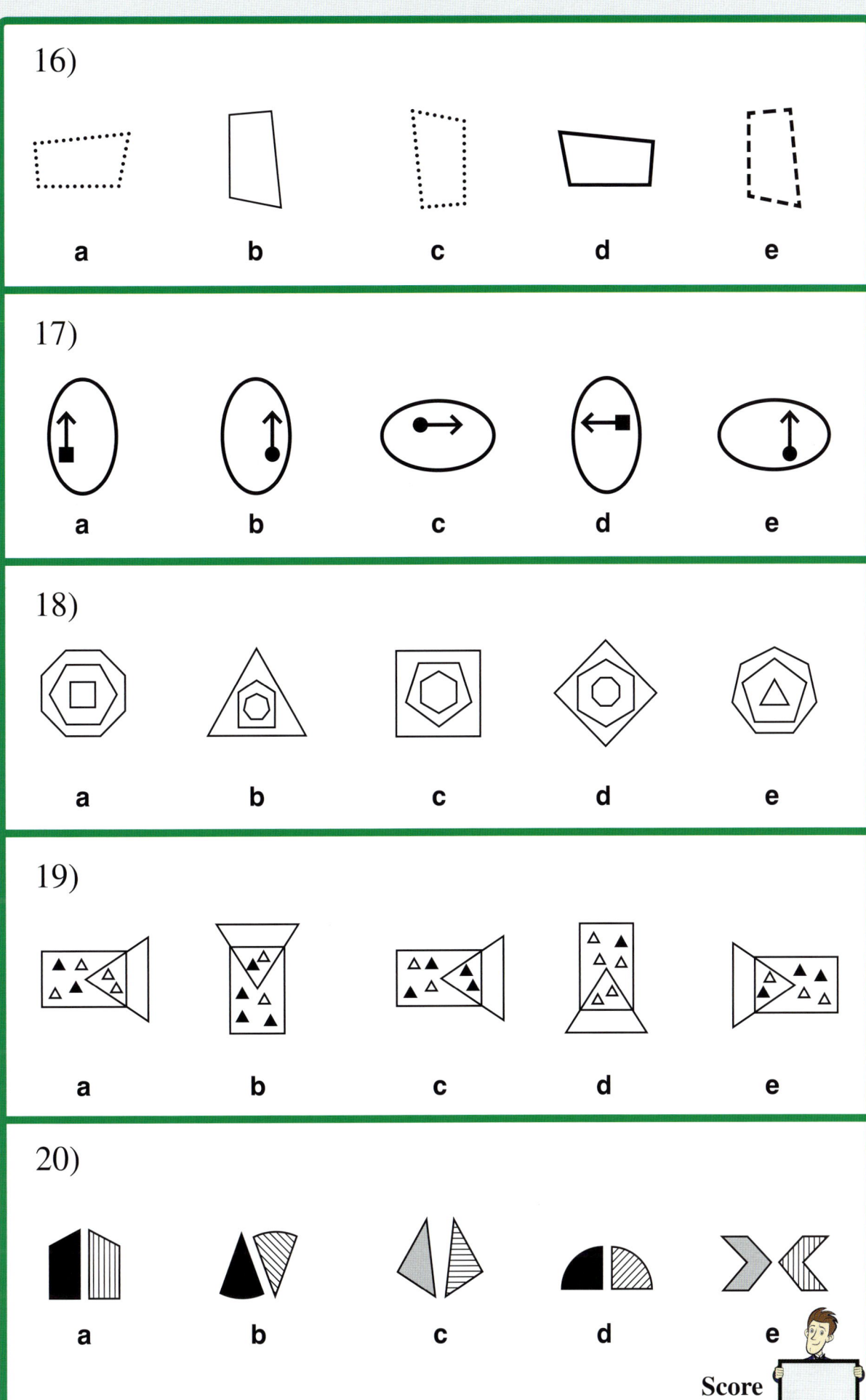

3. Advanced Level

In each of the rows below there are five figures. Find one figure in each row that is **most unlike** the other four.
Example

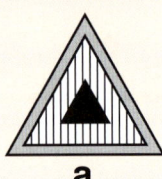 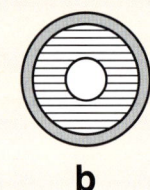 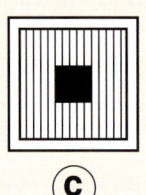 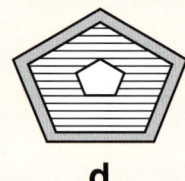 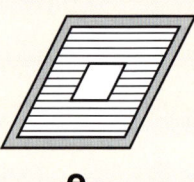

a b c d e

Answer: **c** as it is the only shape that is enclosed by a White border.

Exercise 17: 3 Which figure does not fit in with the others?

1)

 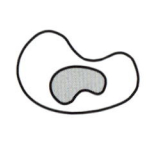  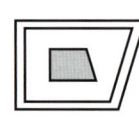 

a b c d e

2)

   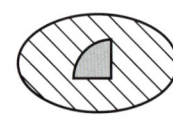 

a b c d e

3)

a b c d e

4)

  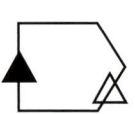 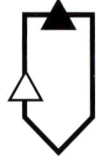 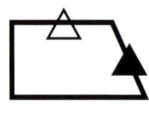

a b c d e

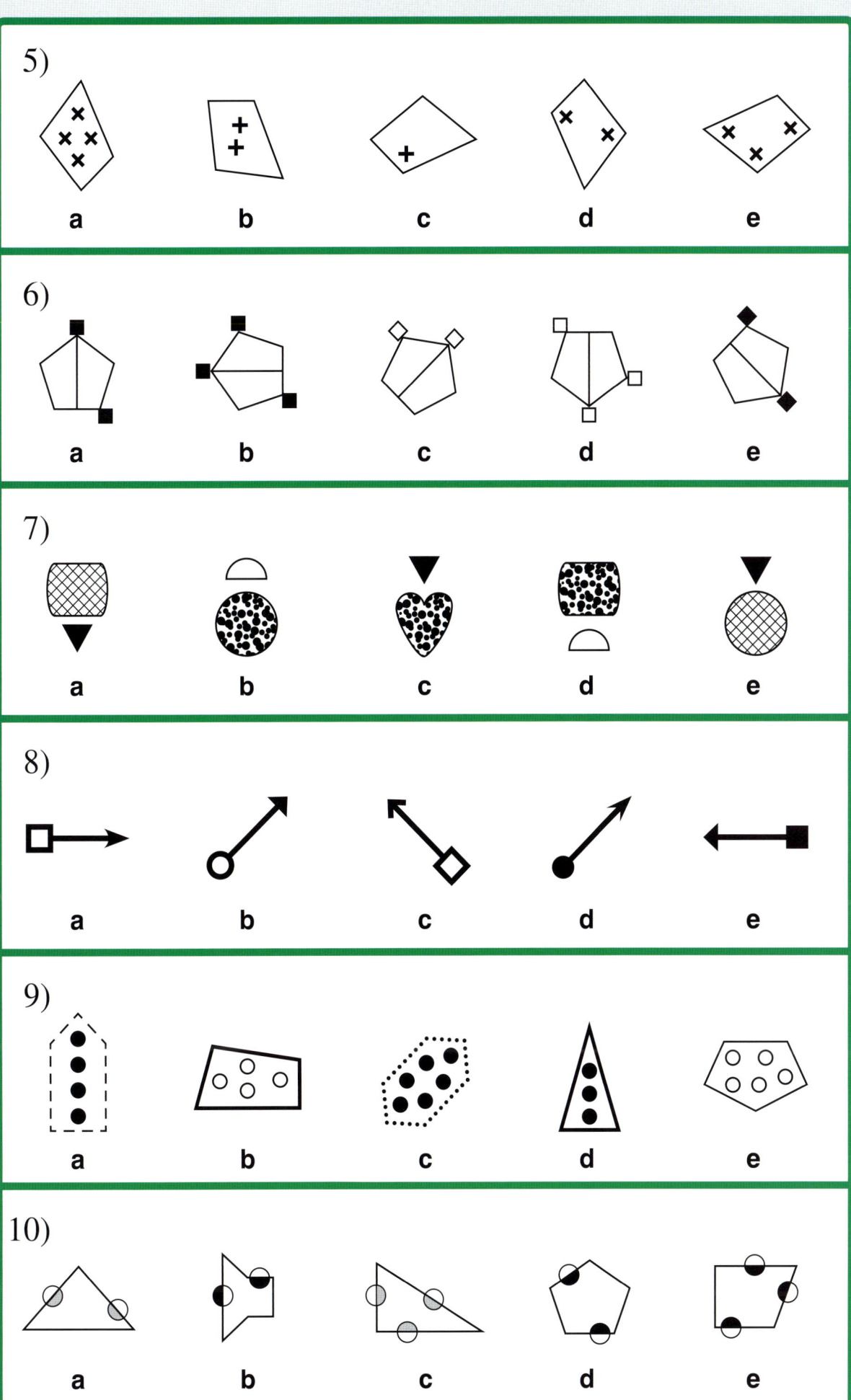

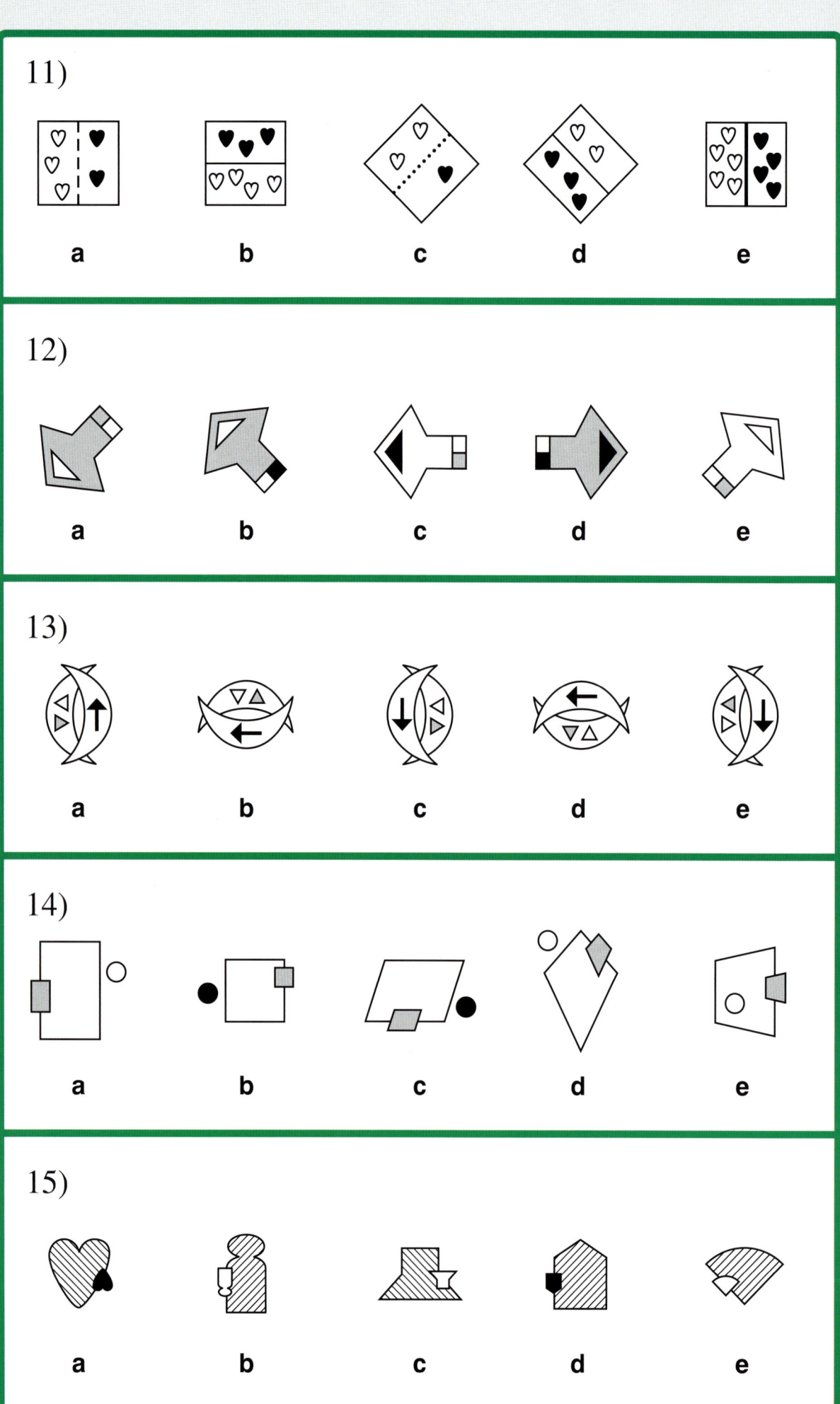

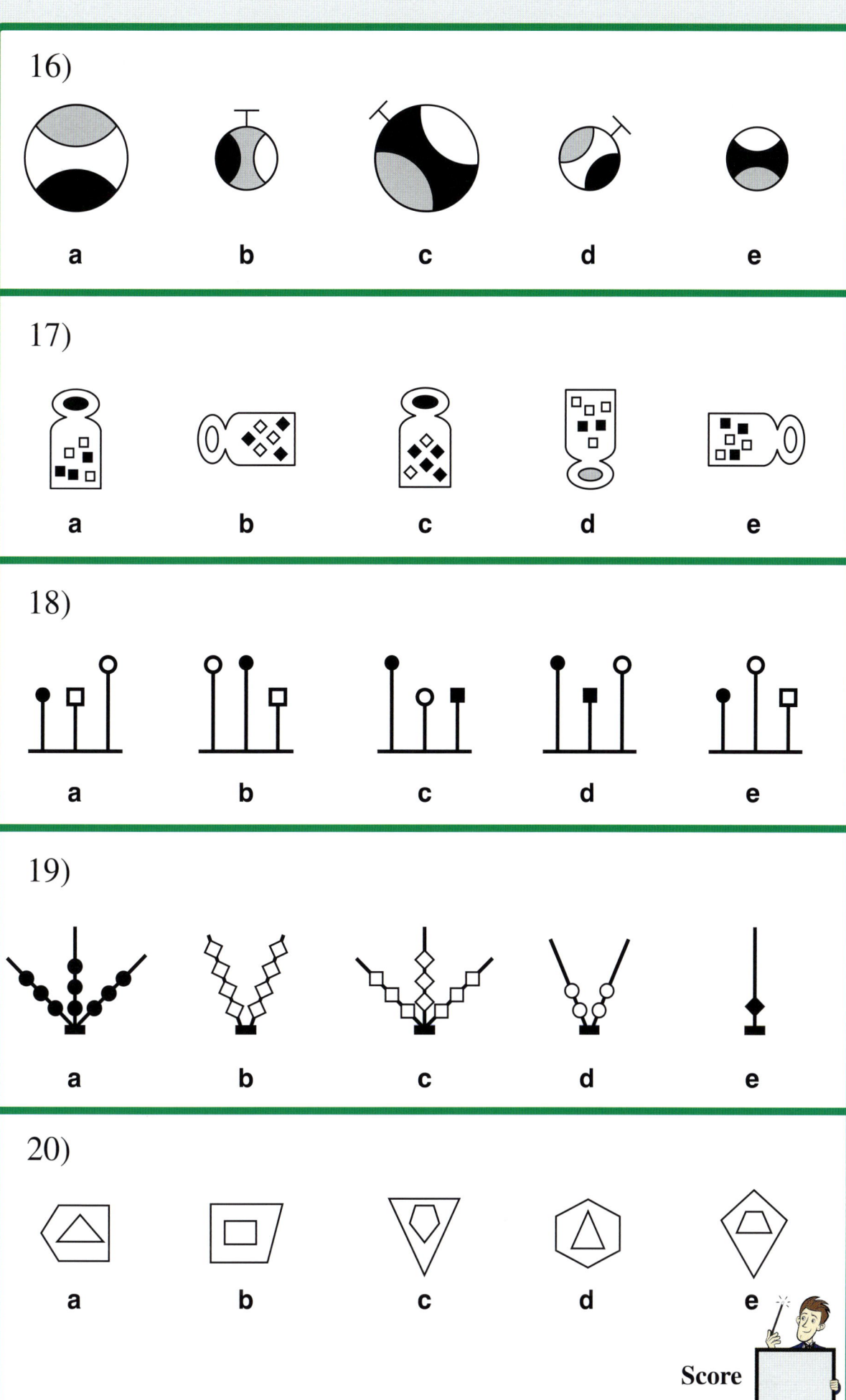

4. Higher Level

In each of the rows below there are five figures. Find one figure in each row that is **most unlike** the other four.

Example

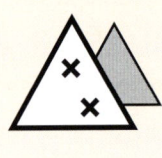  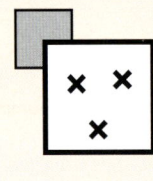  

a   ⓑ   c   d   e

Answer: **b** as there should be one less Cross than the number of sides in the shape.

Exercise 17: 4 Which figure does not fit in with the others?

1)

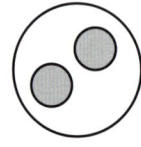 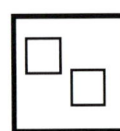   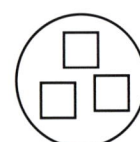

a   b   c   d   e

2)

  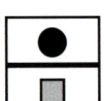 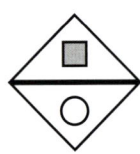 

a   b   c   d   e

3)

 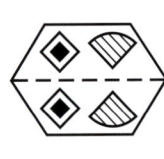  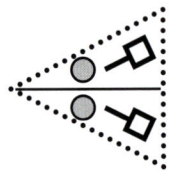 

a   b   c   d   e

4)

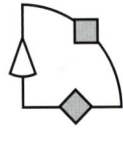  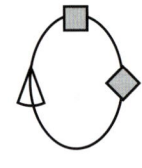 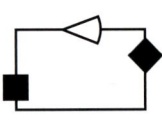 

a   b   c   d   e

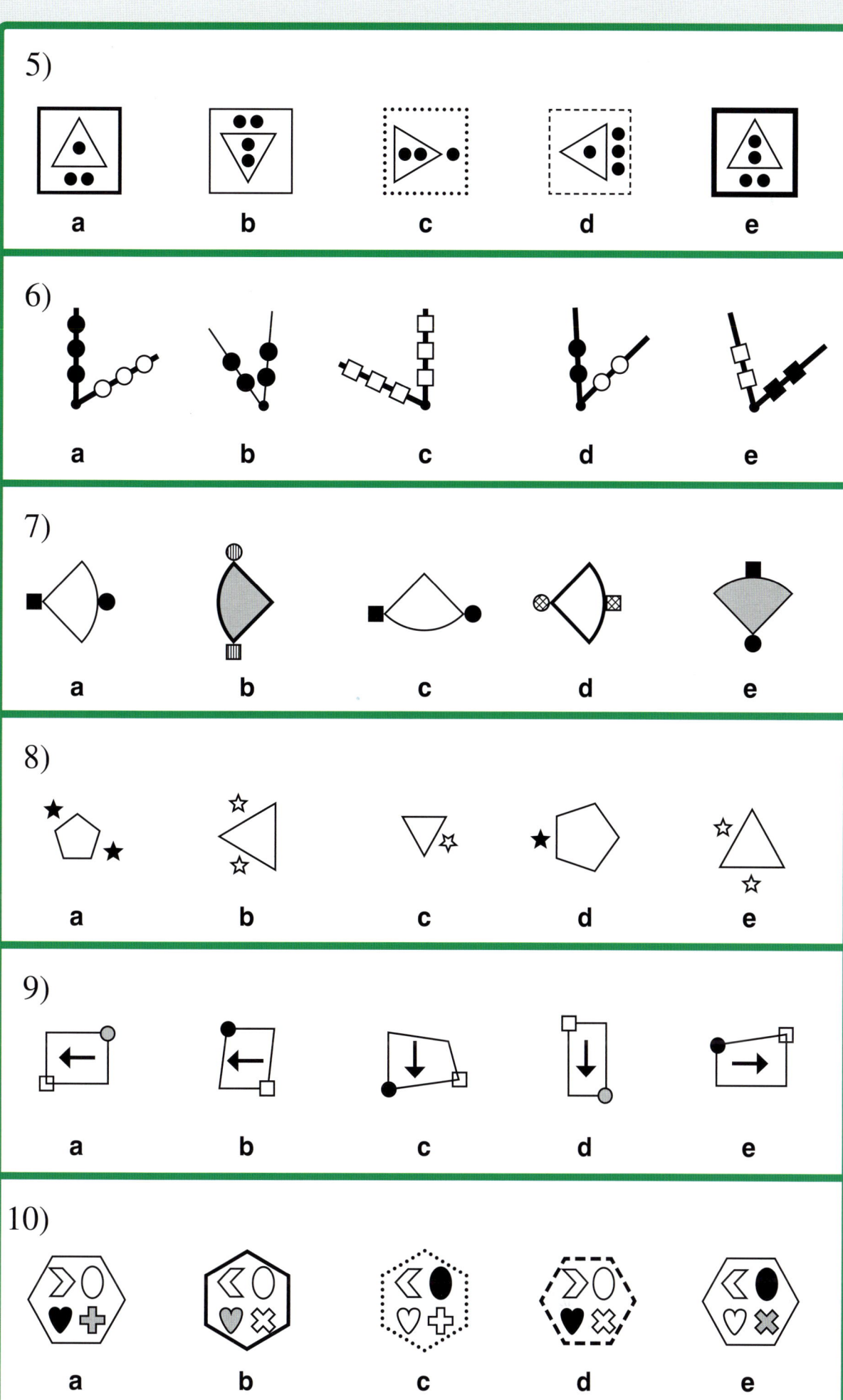

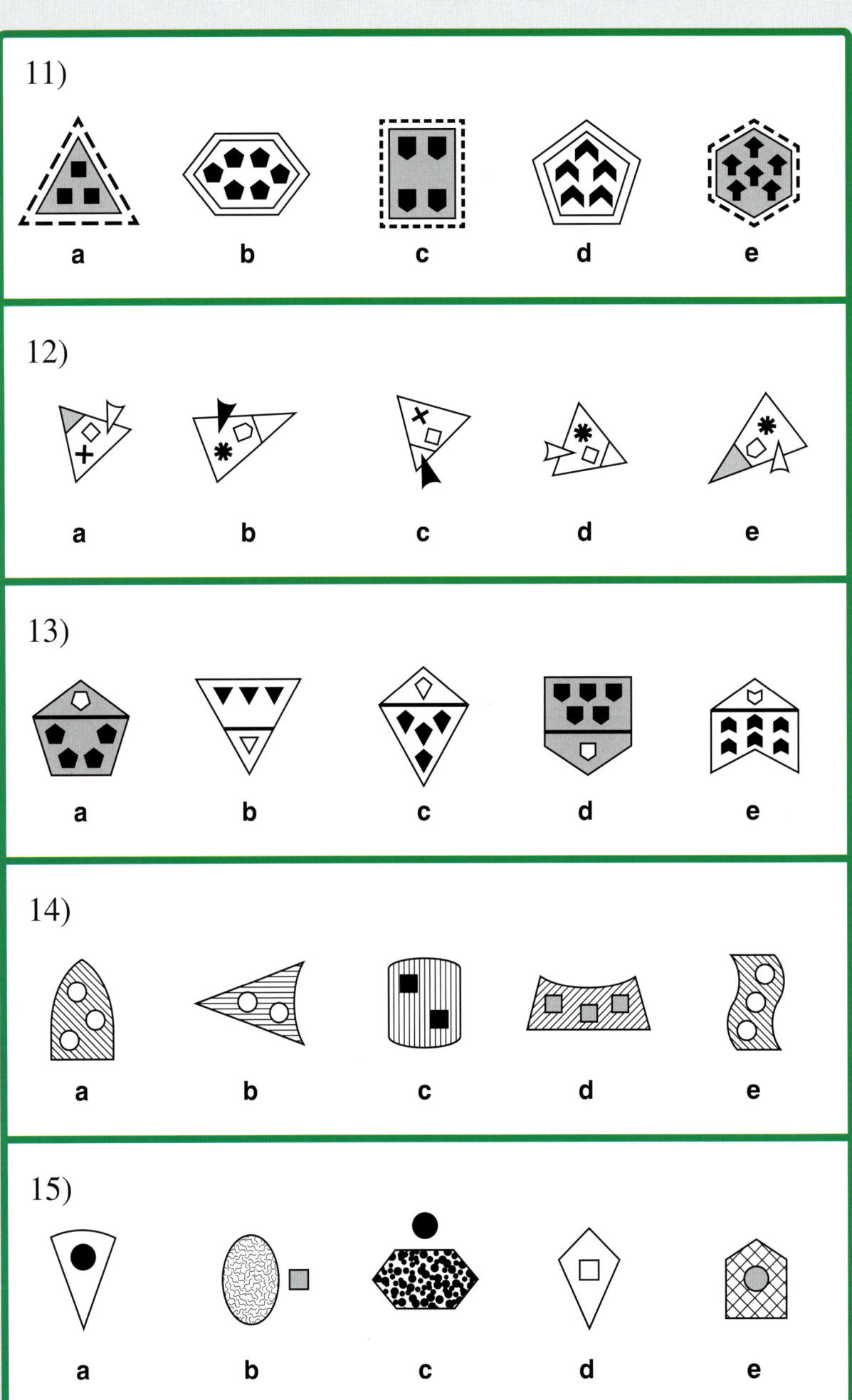

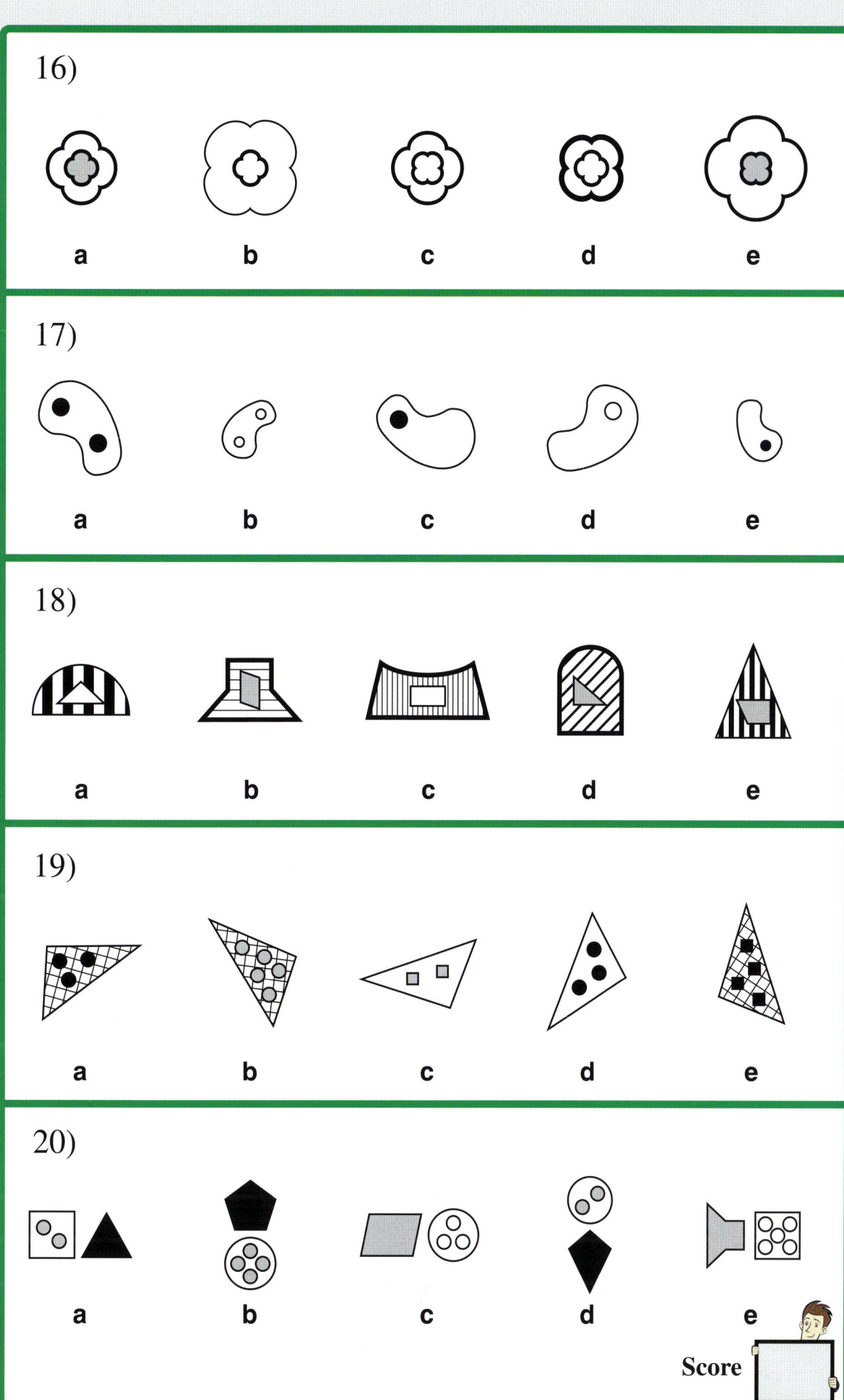

5. Mixed Levels

Exercise 17: 5 Which figure does not fit in with the others?

1)

a　　　　　b　　　　　c　　　　　d　　　　　e

2)

  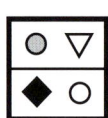 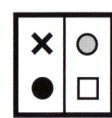 

a　　　　　b　　　　　c　　　　　d　　　　　e

3)

    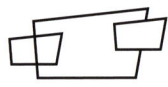

a　　　　　b　　　　　c　　　　　d　　　　　e

4)

 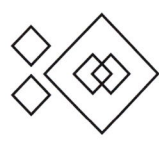   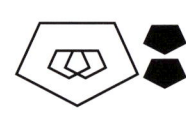

a　　　　　b　　　　　c　　　　　d　　　　　e

5)

a　　　　　b　　　　　c　　　　　d　　　　　e

© 2011 Stephen Curran

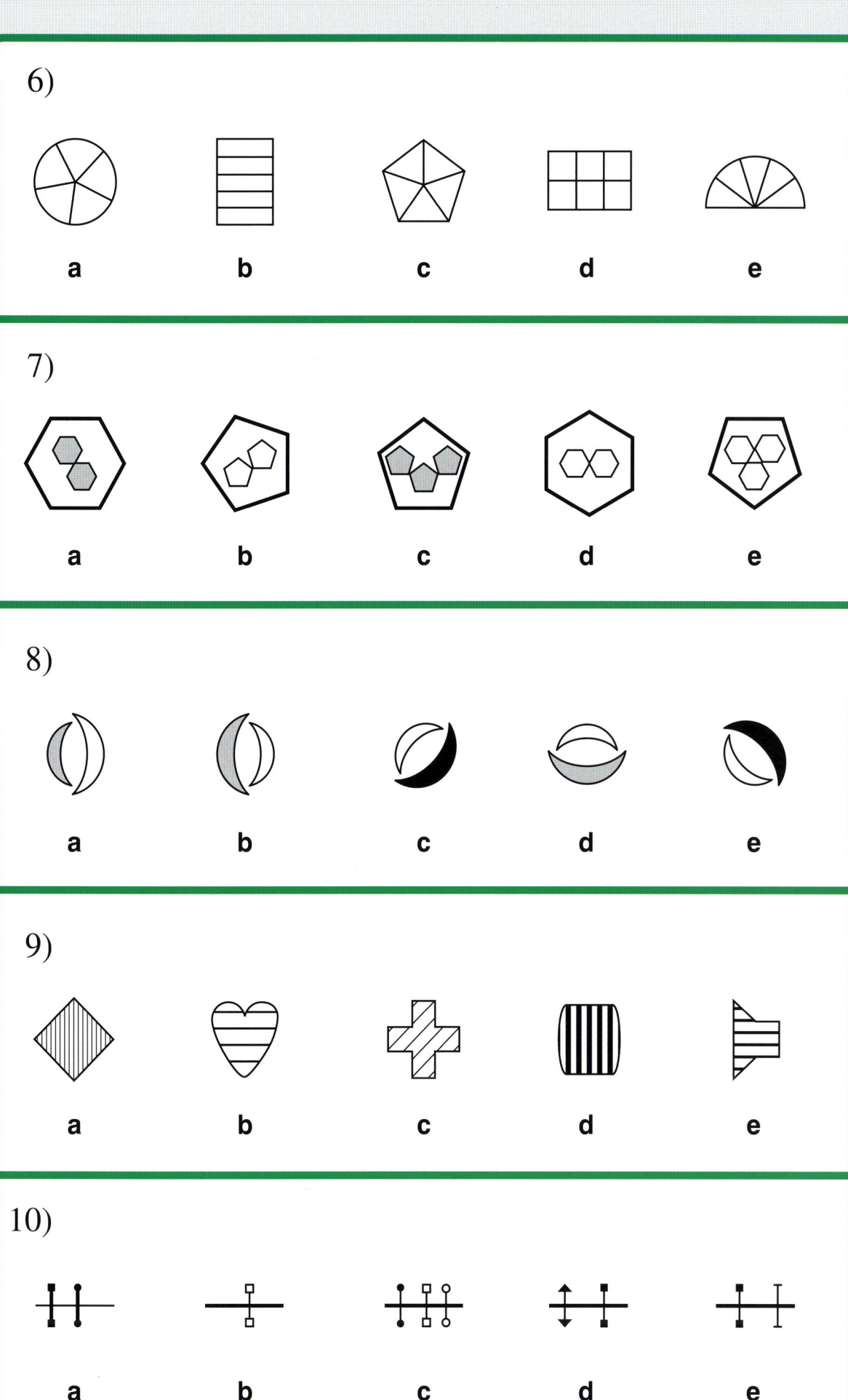

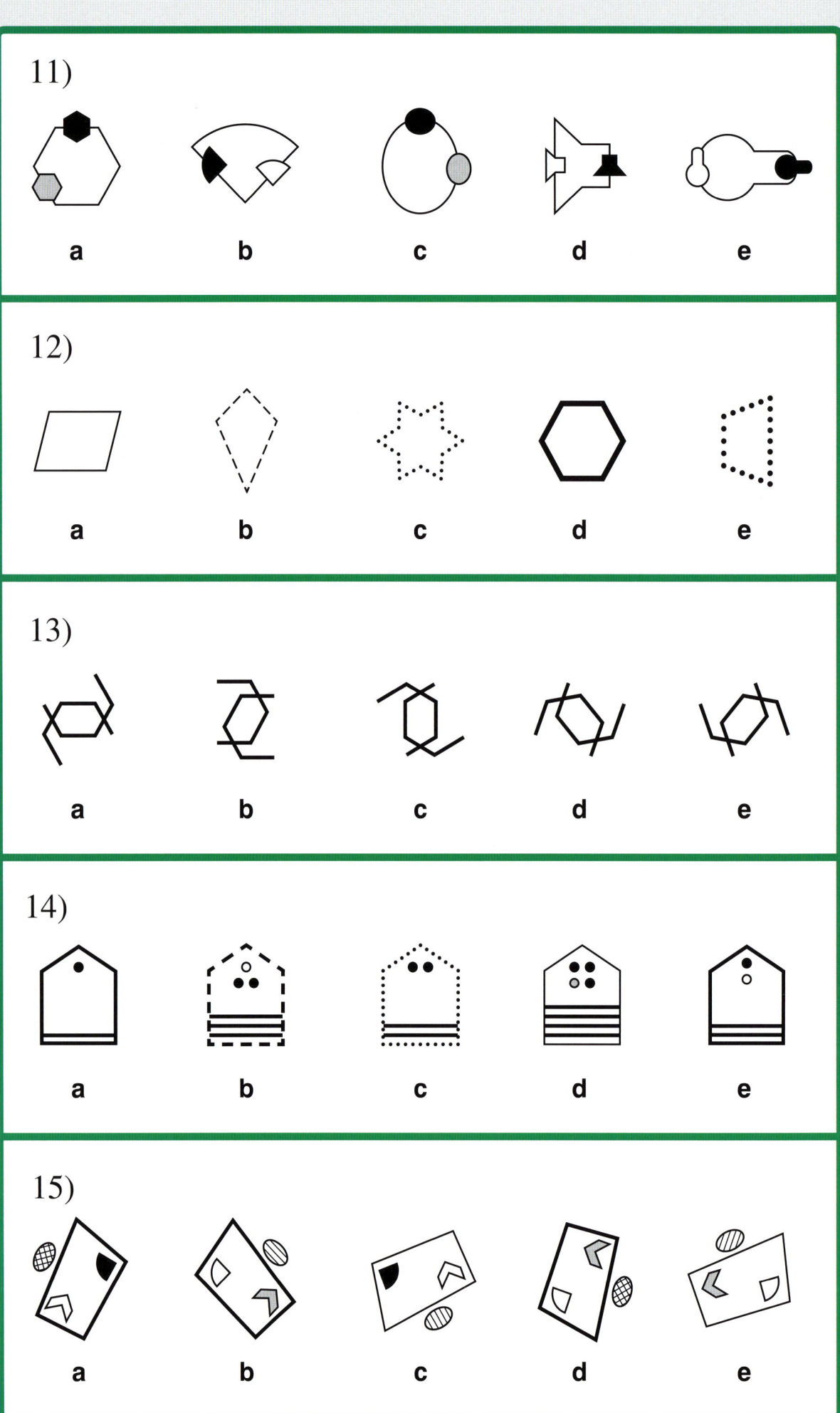

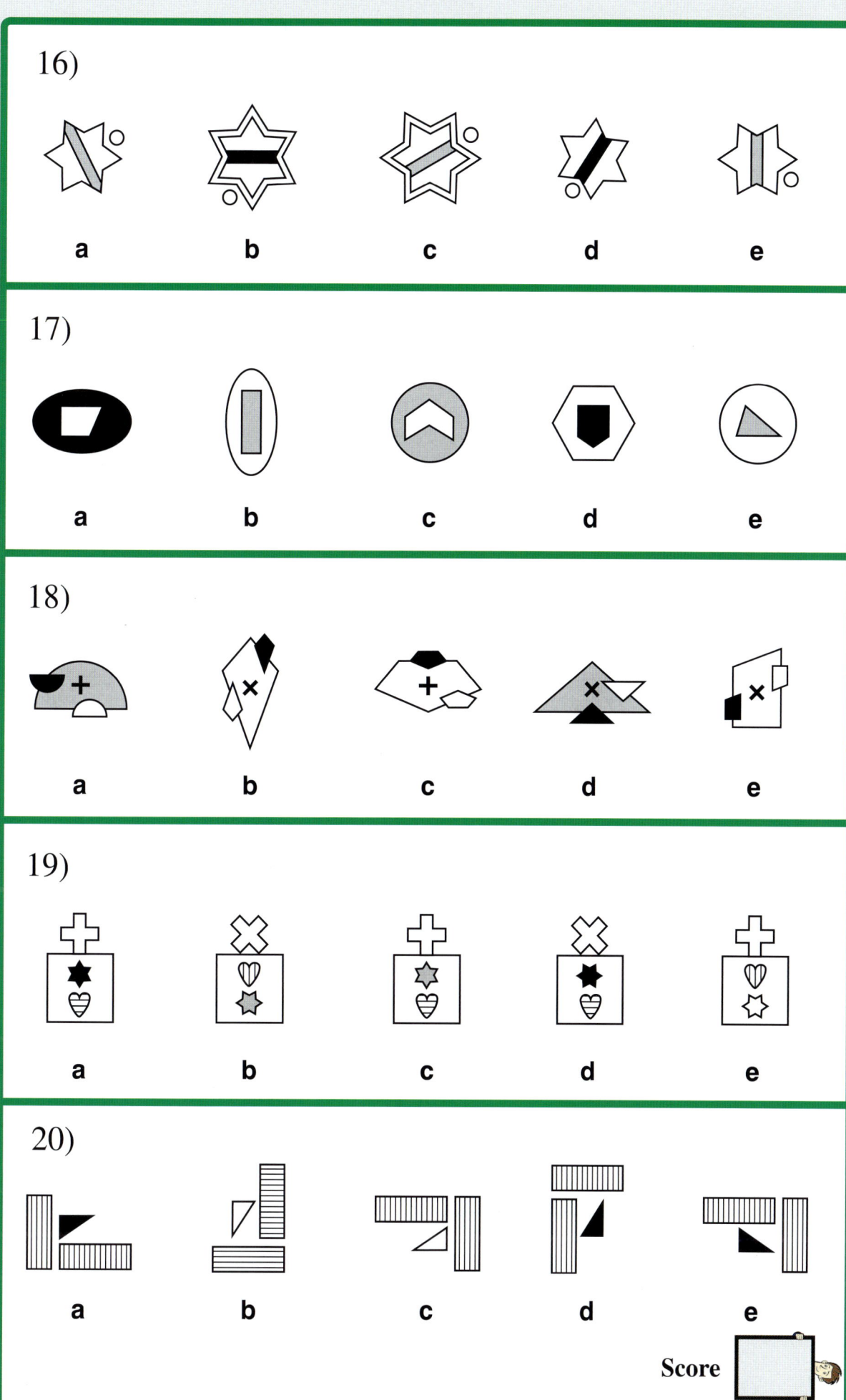

Chapter Eighteen
CODES
1. Type 1 - Level Two

The following figures correspond to the codes below them. Decide how the code letters go with the figures and then find the correct code for the Test Figure.

Example — TEST FIGURE

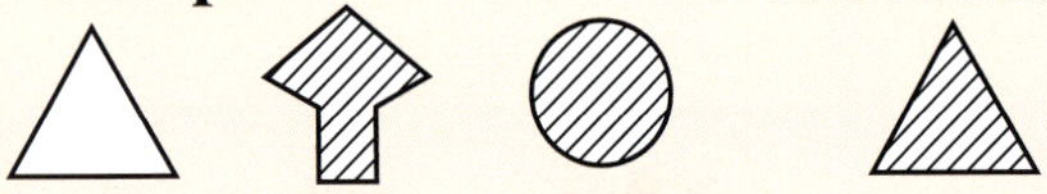

AR, BS, BT — Test Figure
BR (a), AS (b), AT (c), BS (d), AR (e)

The **first letter** stands for the type of fill: **A** - White Fill; **B** - Shaded Fill.
The **second letter** stands for each shape: **R** - Triangle; **S** - Arrow; **T** - Circle.
The answer is **BR**: B for Shaded Fill; R for Triangle.

Exercise 18: 1 Find the code of the Test Figure.

1) HP, JQ, KP — TEST FIGURE
   KQ (a), HP (b), KP (c), JP (d), HQ (e)

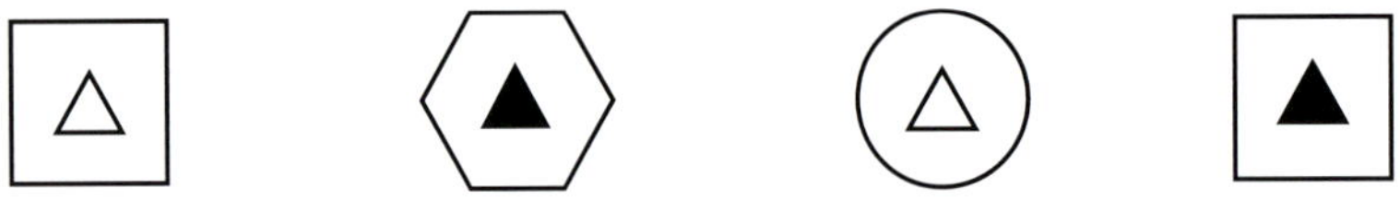

2) SE, TF, SG — TEST FIGURE
   SF (a), TG (b), SG (c), TE (d), GT (e)

3) AZ, BY, AX — TEST FIGURE
   BX (a), ZY (b), BZ (c), AY (d), AB (e)

4) CM, DN, EM — TEST FIGURE
   DM (a), MN (b), EN (c), CM (d), CN (e)

24 © 2011 Stephen Curran

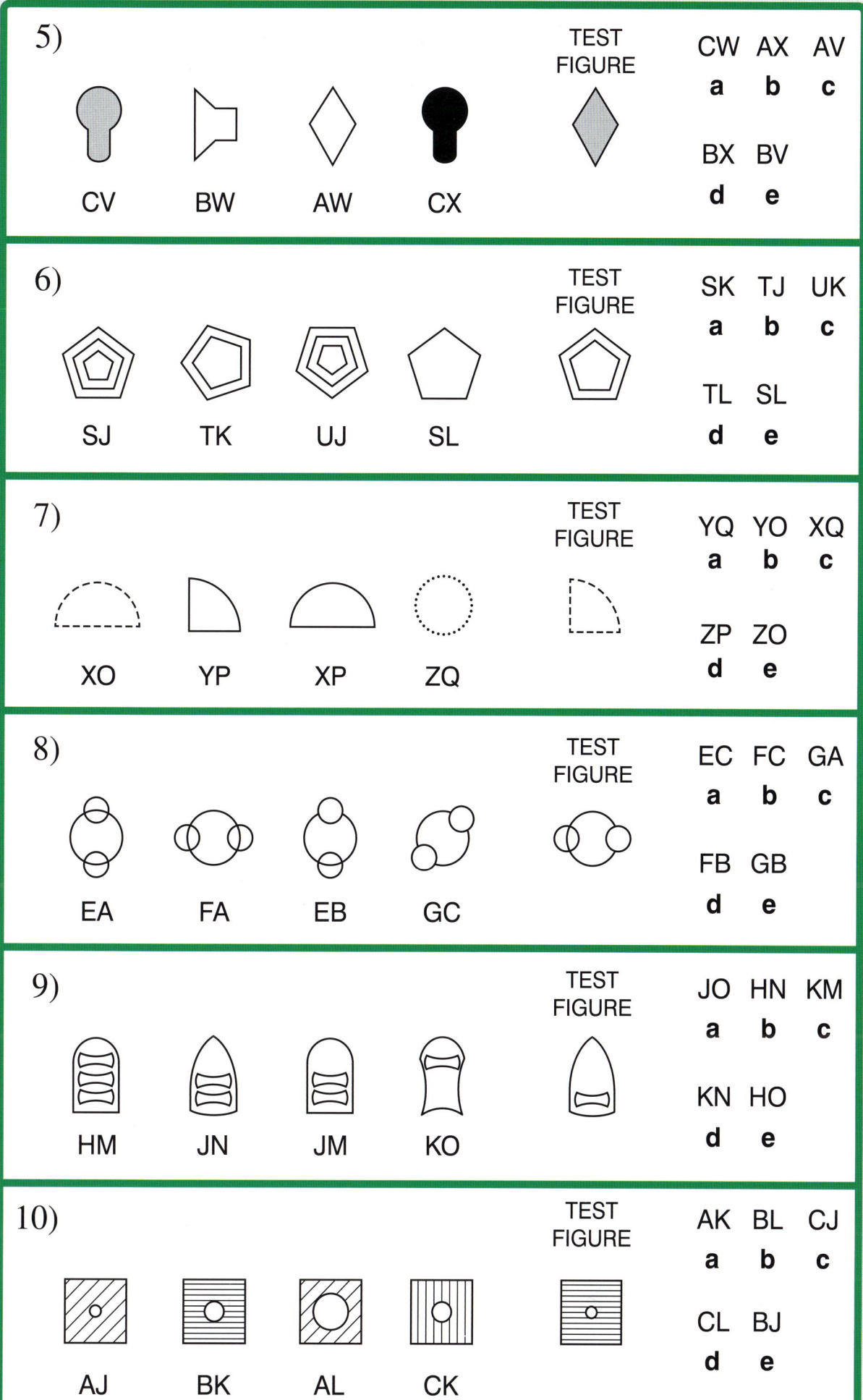

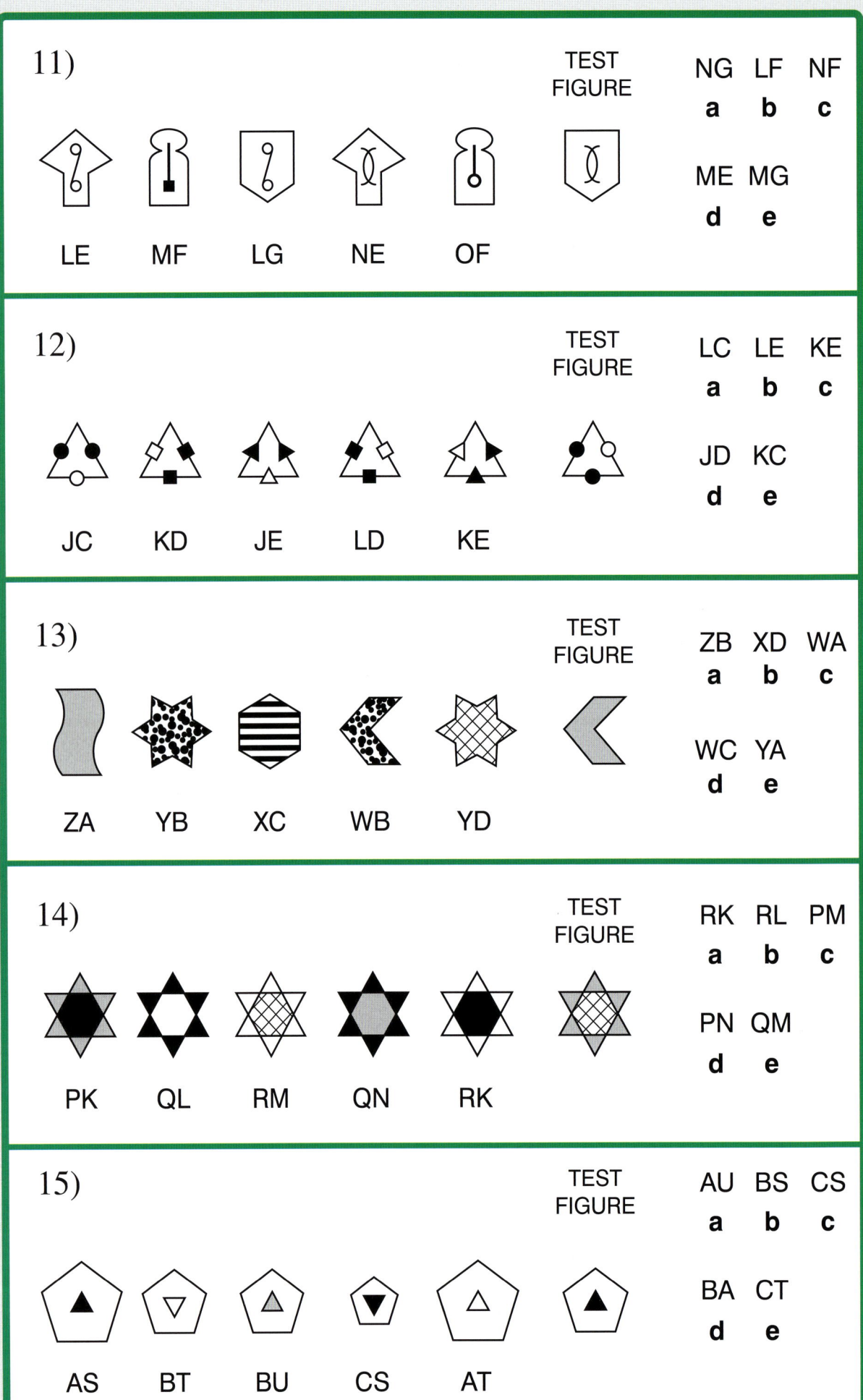

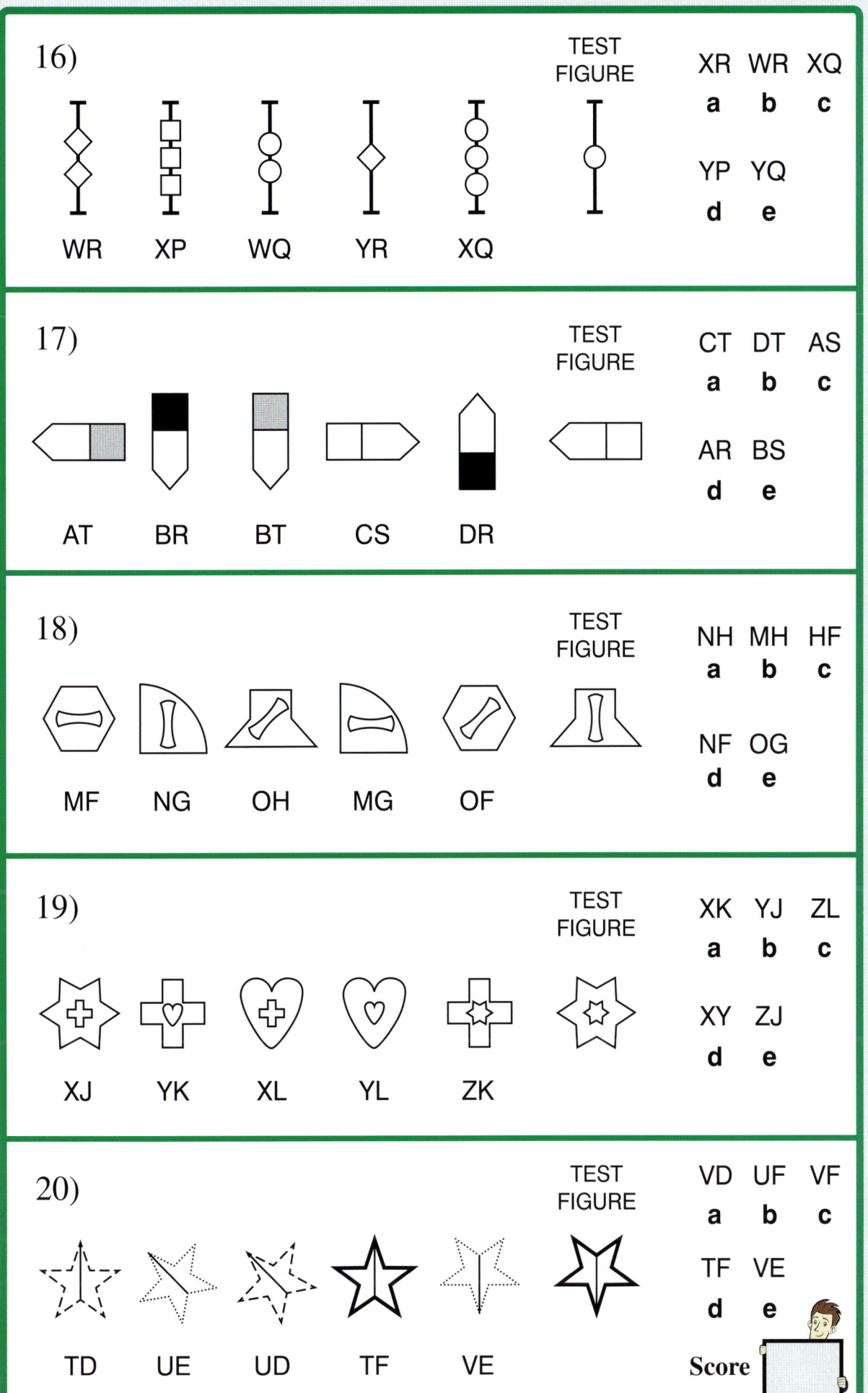

2. Type 2 - Level Two

The following figures correspond to the codes next to them. Decide how the code letters go with the figures and then find the correct code for the Test Figure.

Example

  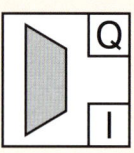  TEST FIGURE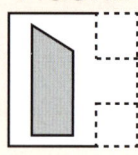

a b c d e

The **top letter** stands for each shape: **Q** - Isosceles Trapezium Shape; **R** - Ordinary Trapezium Shape. The **bottom letter** stands for the type of fill: **H** - White Fill; **I** - Grey Fill; **J** - Black Fill. The answer is **RI**.

Exercise 18: 2 Find the code of the Test Figure.

1)

 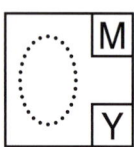 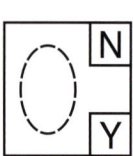  TEST FIGURE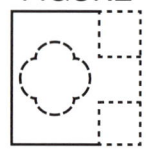

a b c d e

2)

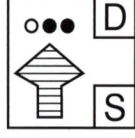    TEST FIGURE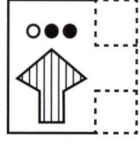

a b c d e

3)

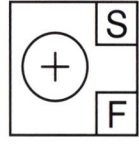 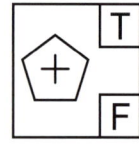 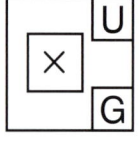 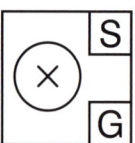 TEST FIGURE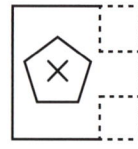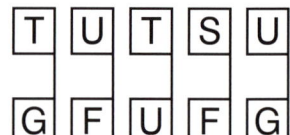

a b c d e

4)

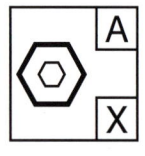 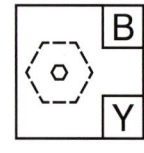 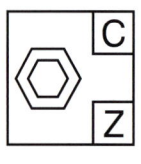 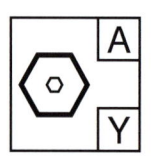 TEST FIGURE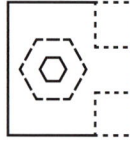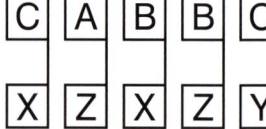

a b c d e

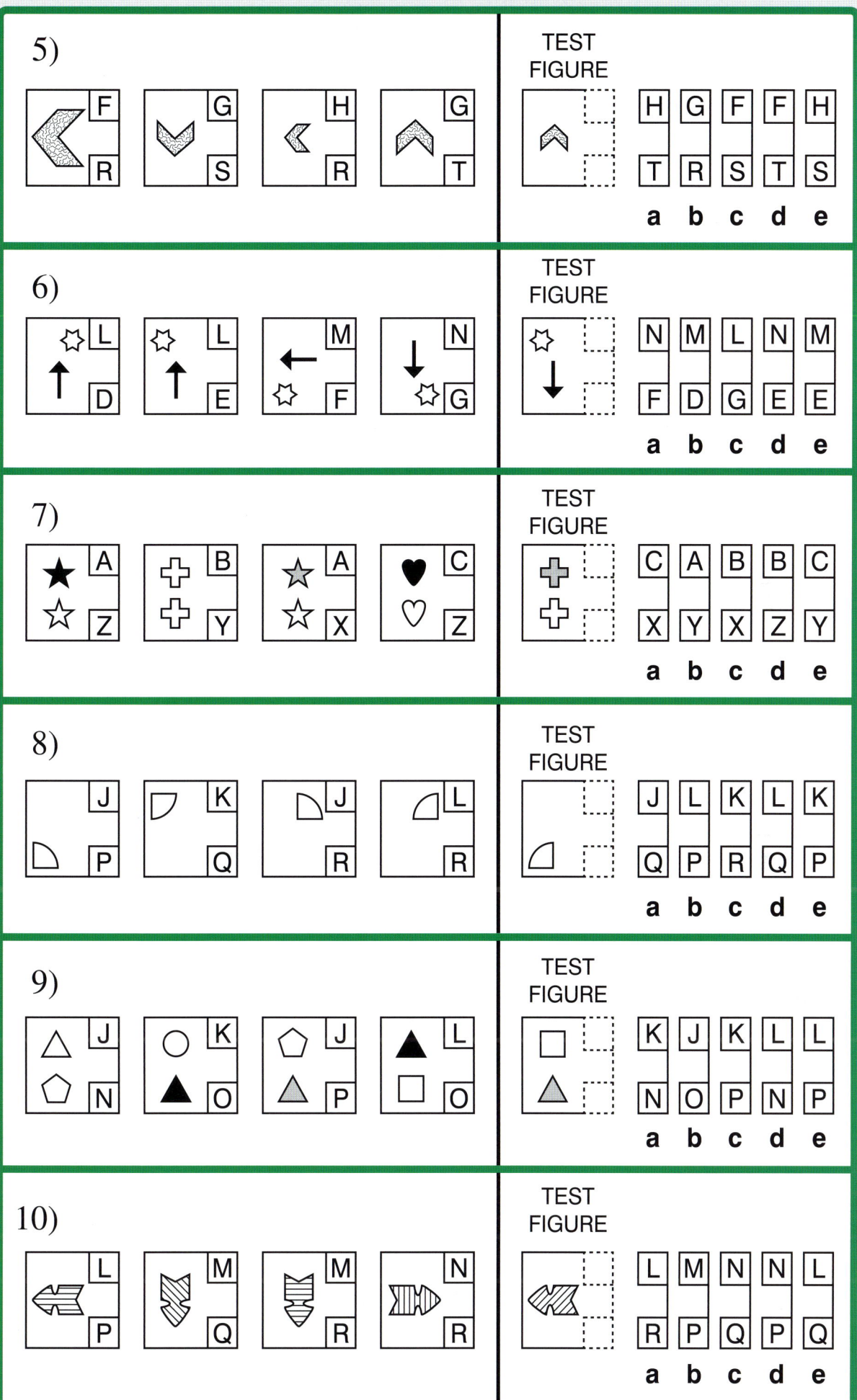

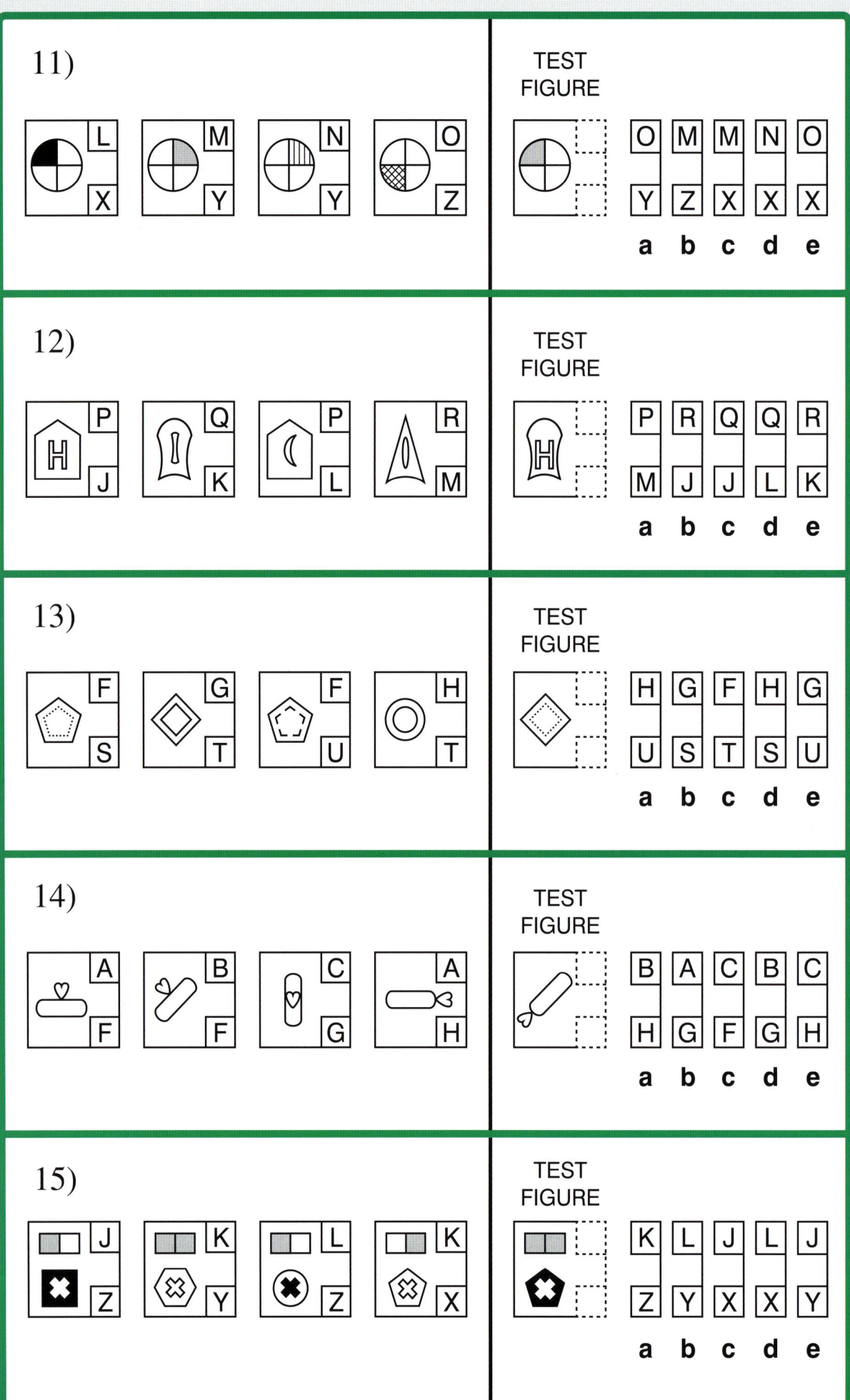

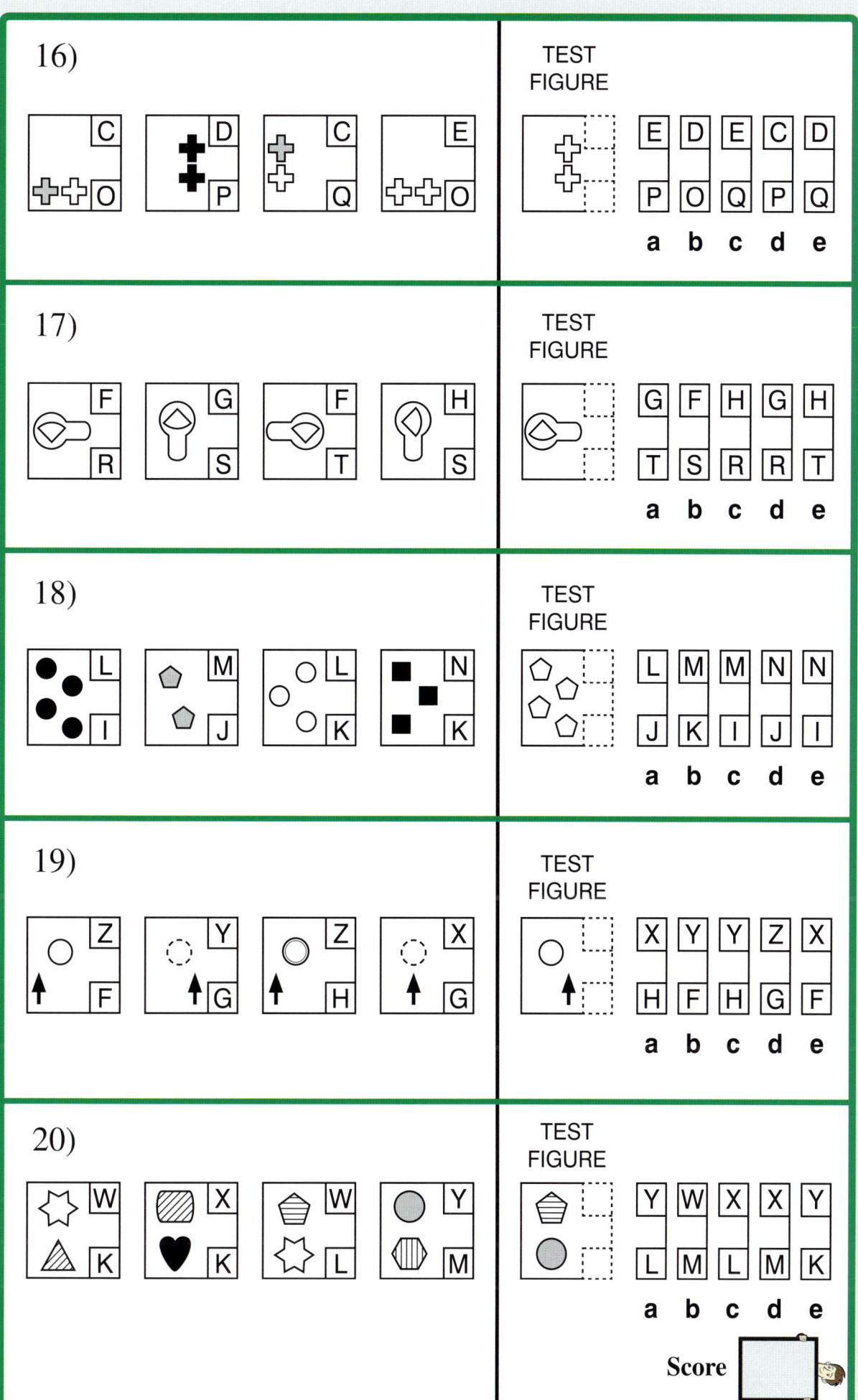

3. Type 1 - Level Three

The following figures correspond to the codes below them. Decide how the code letters go with the figures and then find the correct code for the Test Figure.

Example   TEST FIGURE

    BRY   ASX   ATX   BRX   ARY
ARX   BSY   BTX   a   b   c   (d)   e

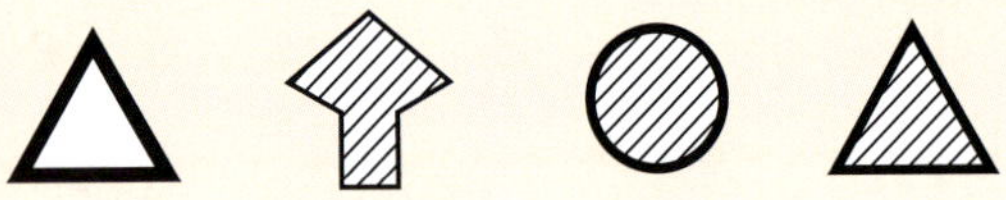

The answer is **d**: **B** stands for Shaded Fill; **R** for Triangle; **X** for Thick Solid Line.

Exercise 18: 3 Find the code of the Test Figure.

1)   ZCG   XDG   ZEH   TEST FIGURE   XCH XEH ZDG
                                             a   b   c
                                           XCG XEG
                                             d   e

2)   PAU   QBV   RAV   TEST FIGURE   RBV PAV PBU
                                             a   b   c
                                           PBV QAU
                                             d   e

3)   KAS   LBS   MAT   TEST FIGURE   KAT KBS KBT
                                             a   b   c
                                           LBT MBS
                                             d   e

4)   XEV   YFW   XGW   TEST FIGURE   XFV YEV YGV
                                             a   b   c
                                           YEW XFW
                                             d   e

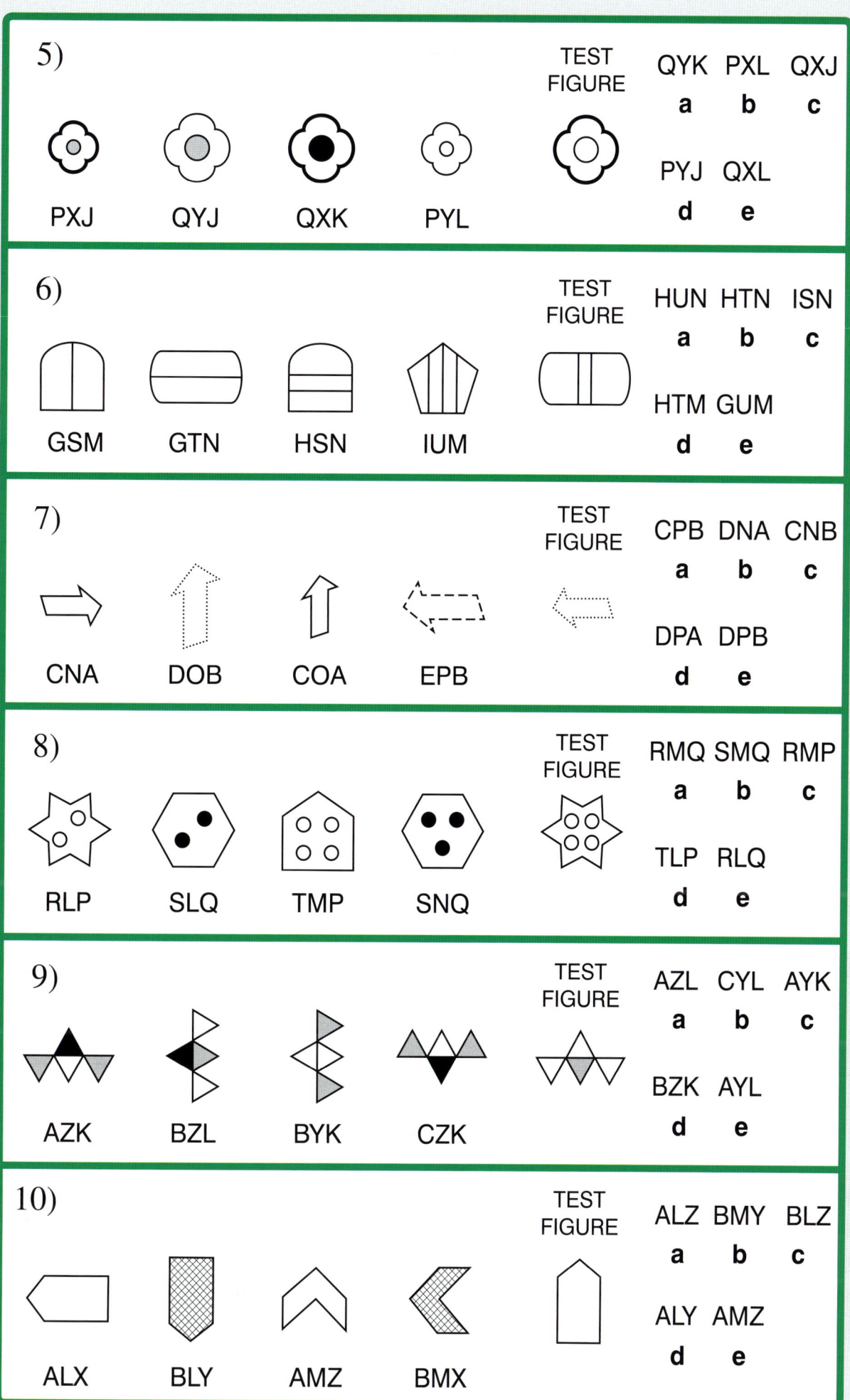

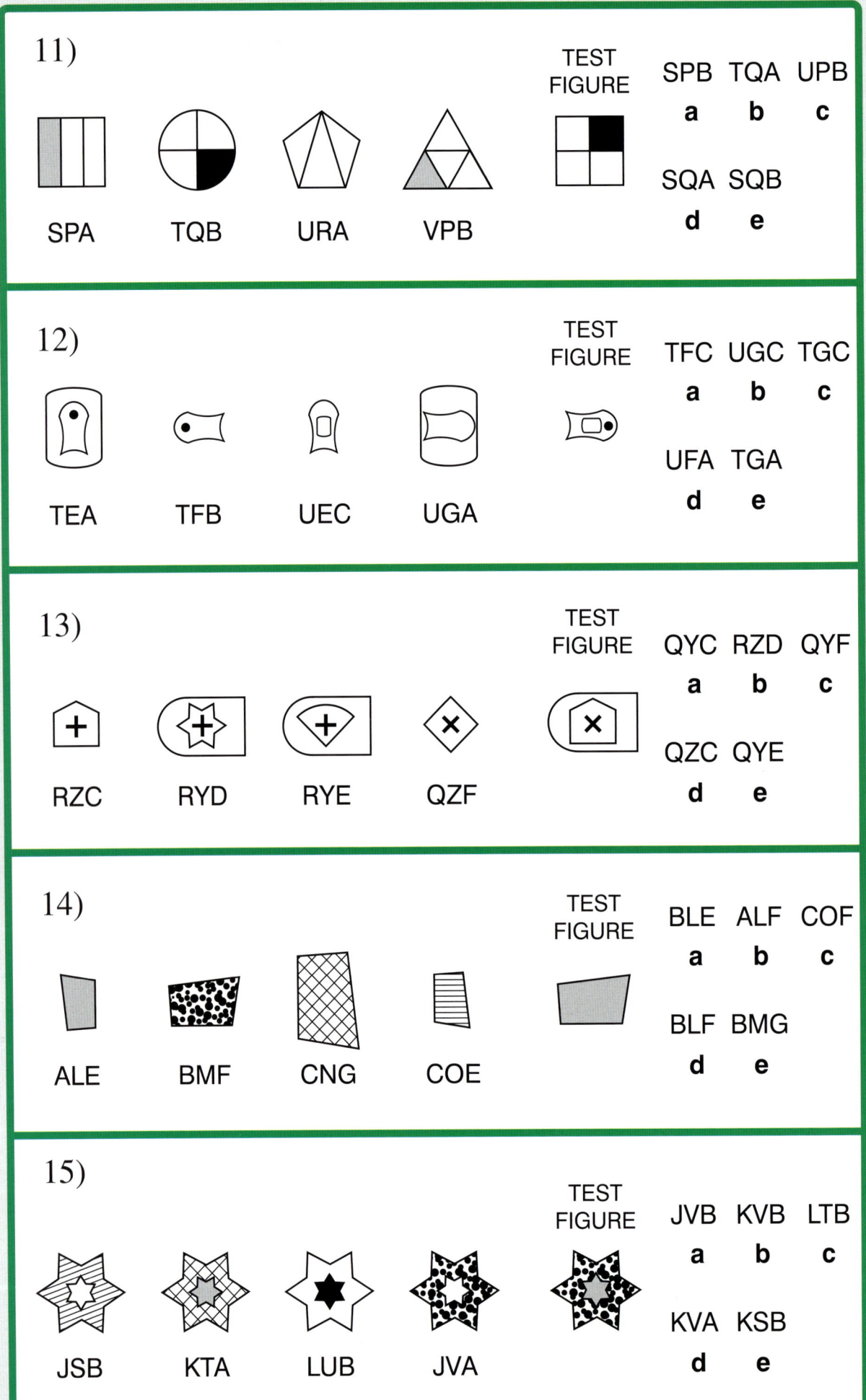

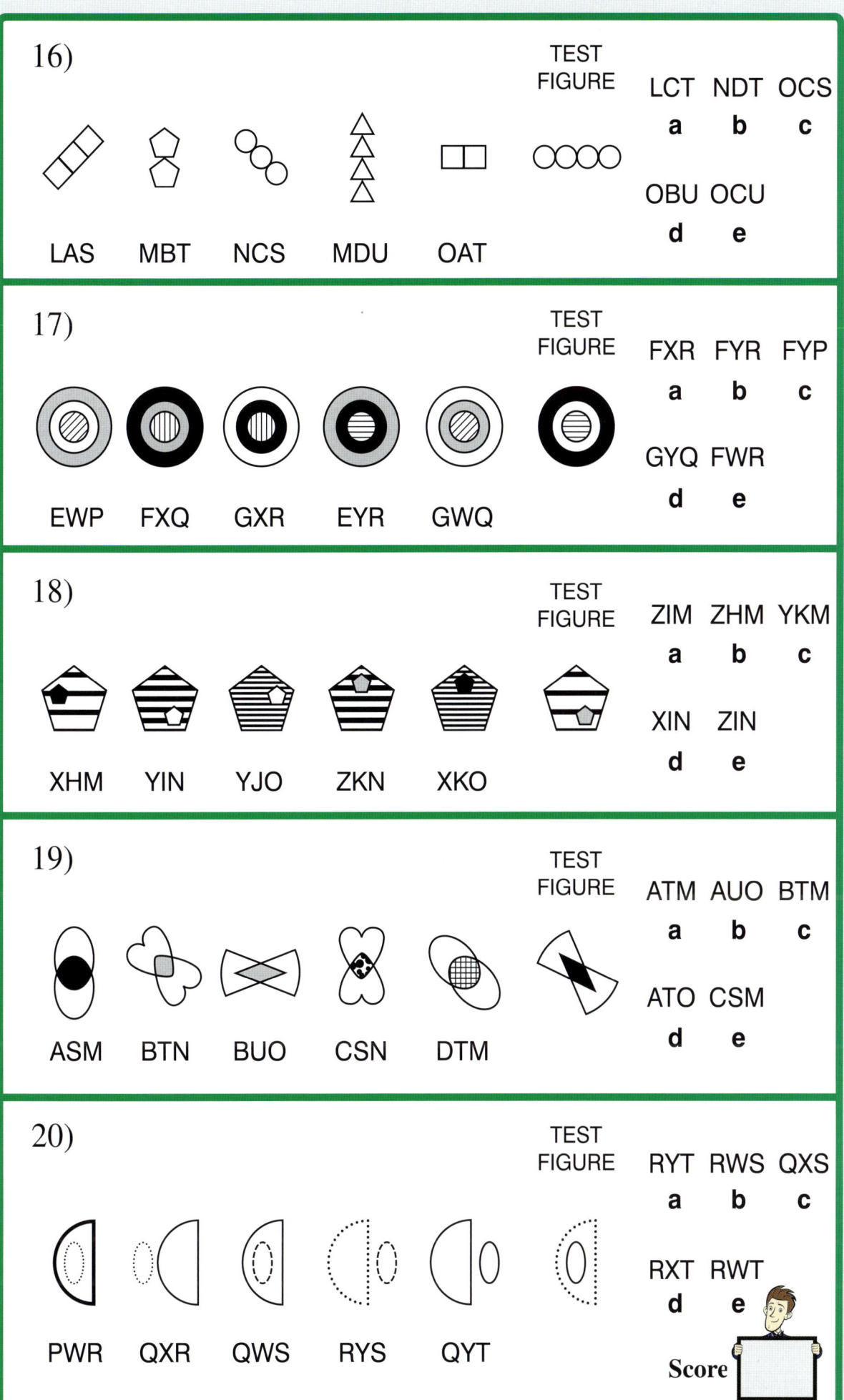

4. Type 1 - Level Four

The following figures correspond to the codes below them. Decide how the code letters go with the figures and then find the correct code for the Test Figure.

Example

TEST FIGURE

    BRXG ASYG ATXF BRYG BRXF
ARXF BSYF BTXG   a   b   c   d   (e)

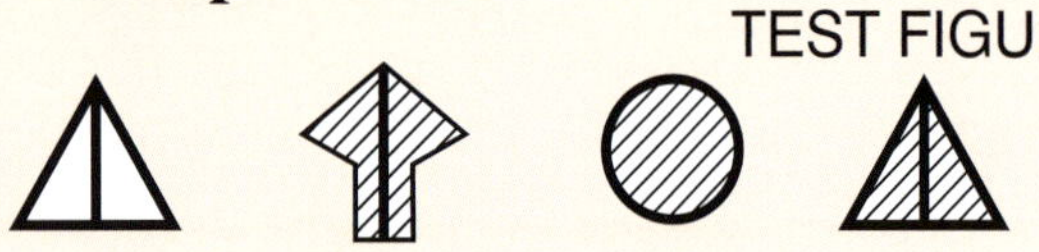

The answer is **e**: **B** stands for Shaded Fill; **R** for Triangle; **X** for Thick Solid Line; **F** for vertical line of symmetry.

Exercise 18: 4 Find the code of the Test Figure.

1)
RXAJ   SYAK   SZBK   RYCL   TEST FIGURE   SXAK SXBJ SYAL
                                             a   b   c
                                            RZCL SXBL
                                             d   e

2)
PECW   QEDV   RFCV   QGDW   TEST FIGURE   REDW PGCV QGCV
                                             a   b   c
                                            PGDV PFCW
                                             d   e

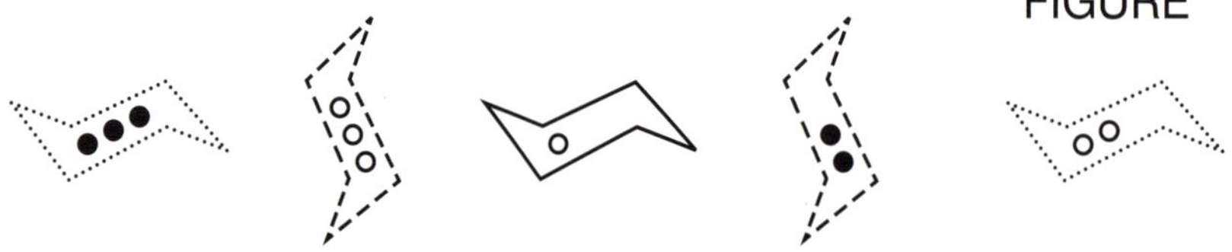

3)
LCRG   MDSH   LETG   MCUF   TEST FIGURE   LDSG MERH MDTH
                                             a   b   c
                                            MEUG MERF
                                             d   e

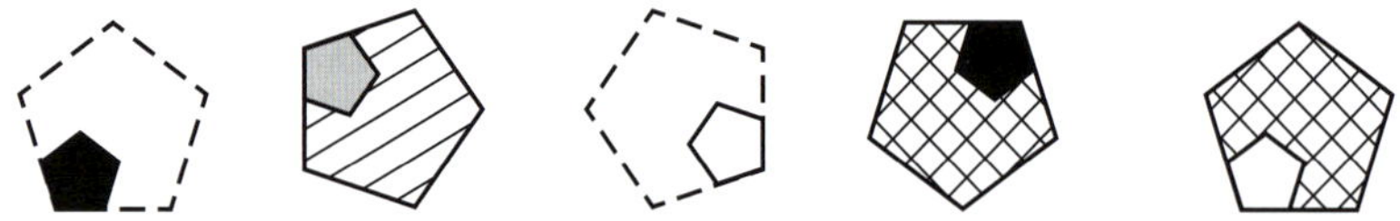

4)
RXAL   SYBM   RYBL   TXCM   TEST FIGURE   TXAM SYCL TXAL
                                             a   b   c
                                            SXCM TYAL
                                             d   e

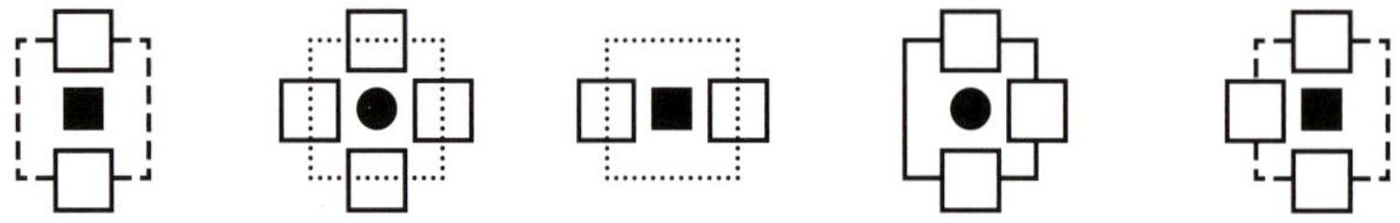

36   © 2011 Stephen Curran

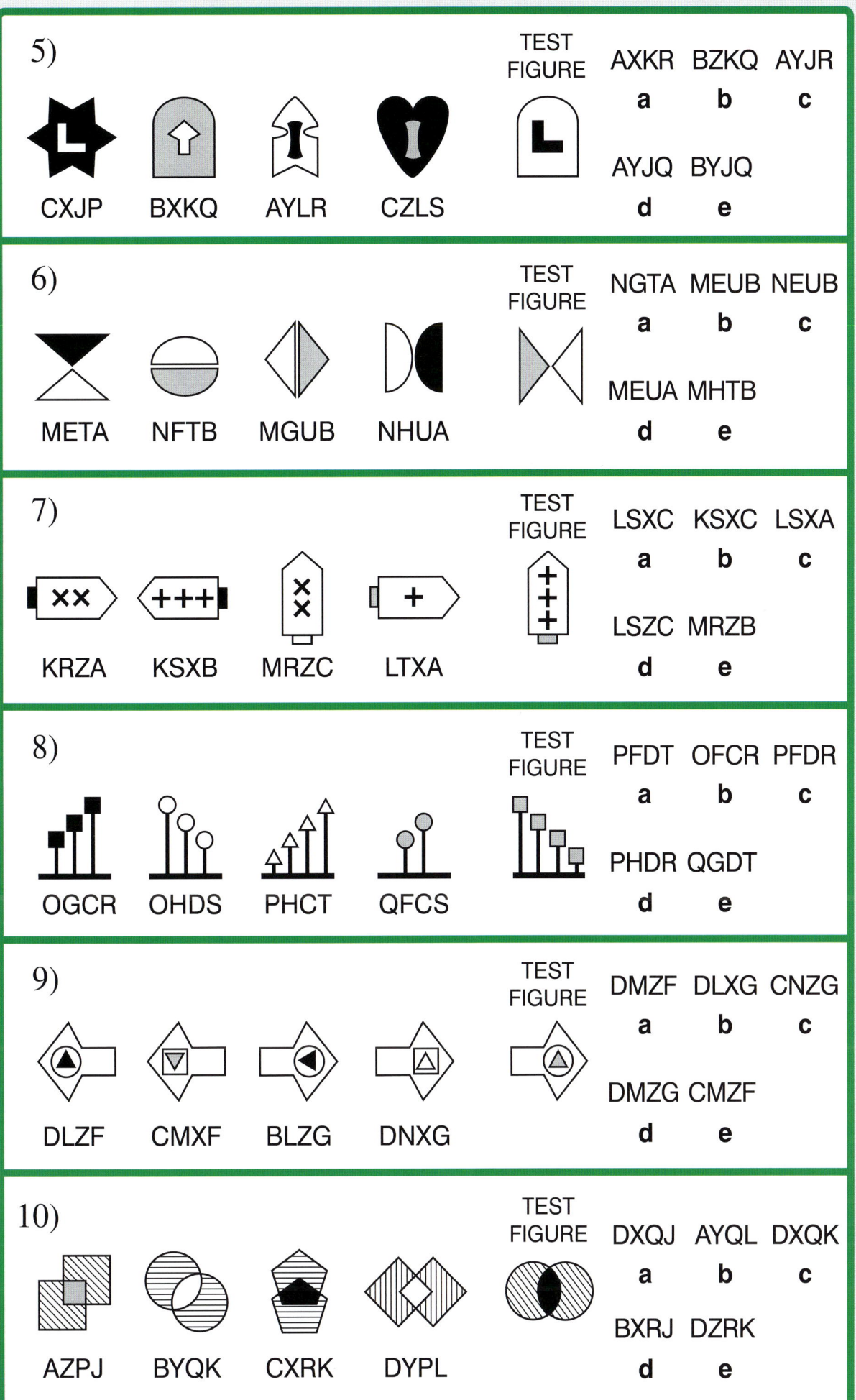

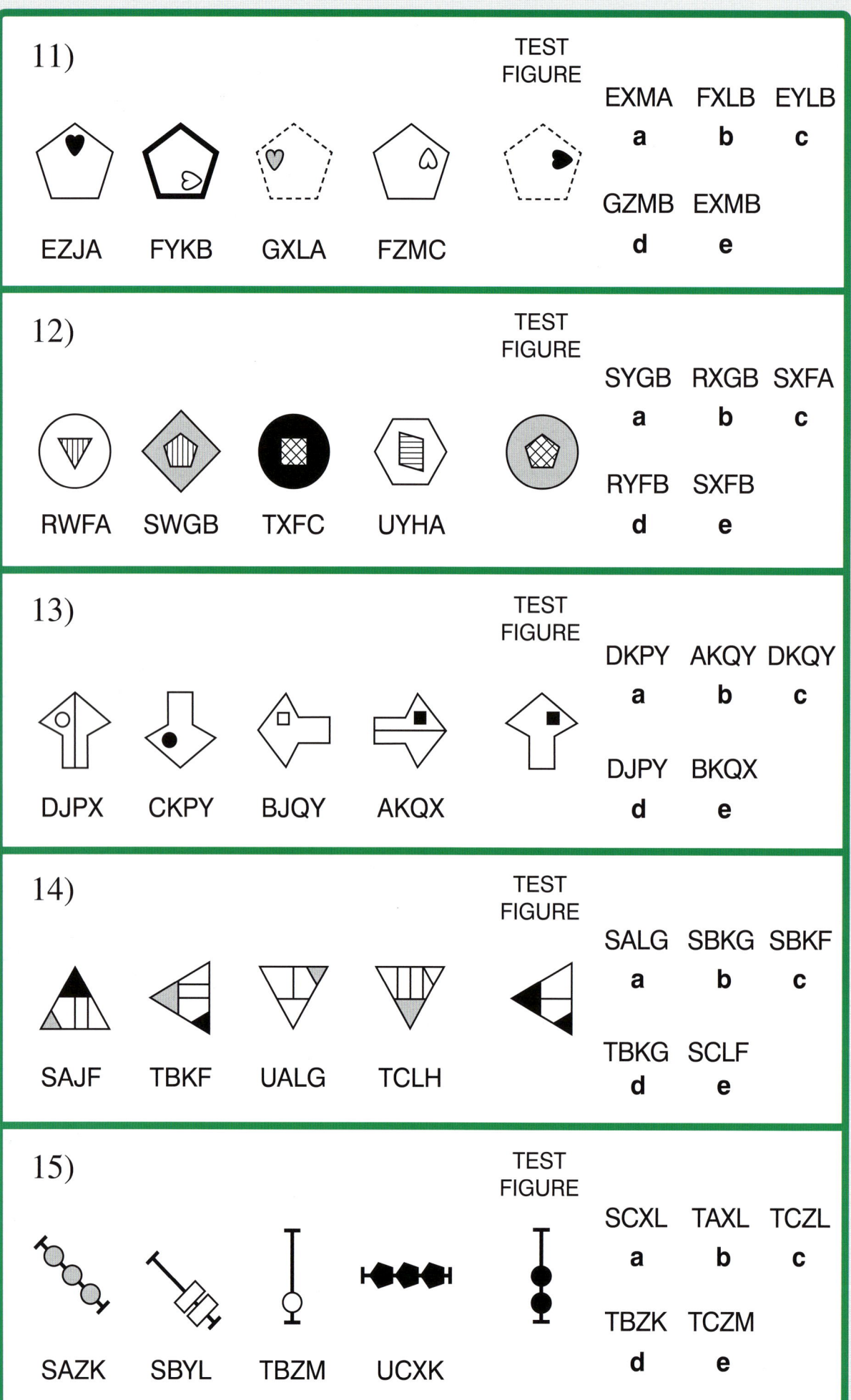

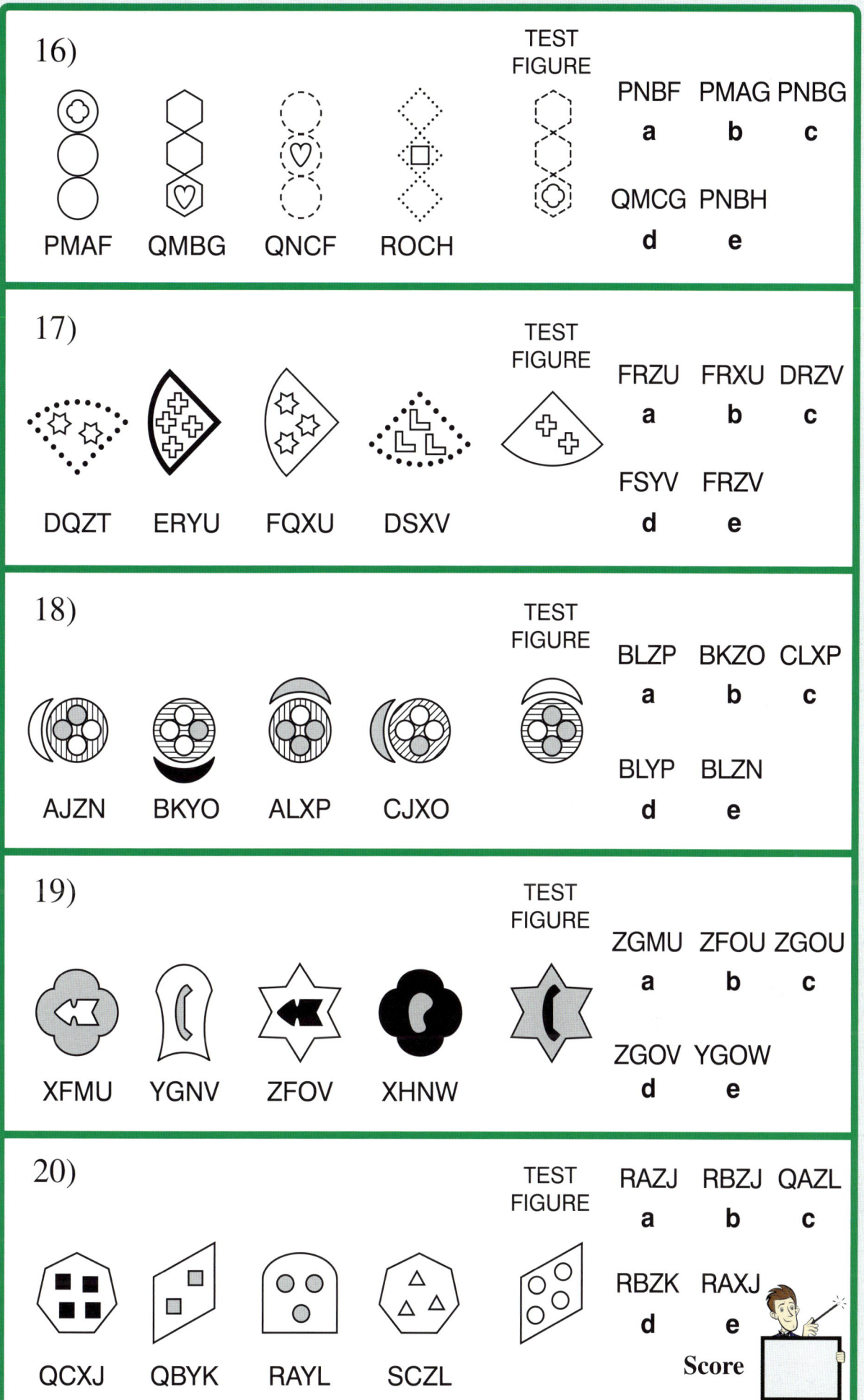

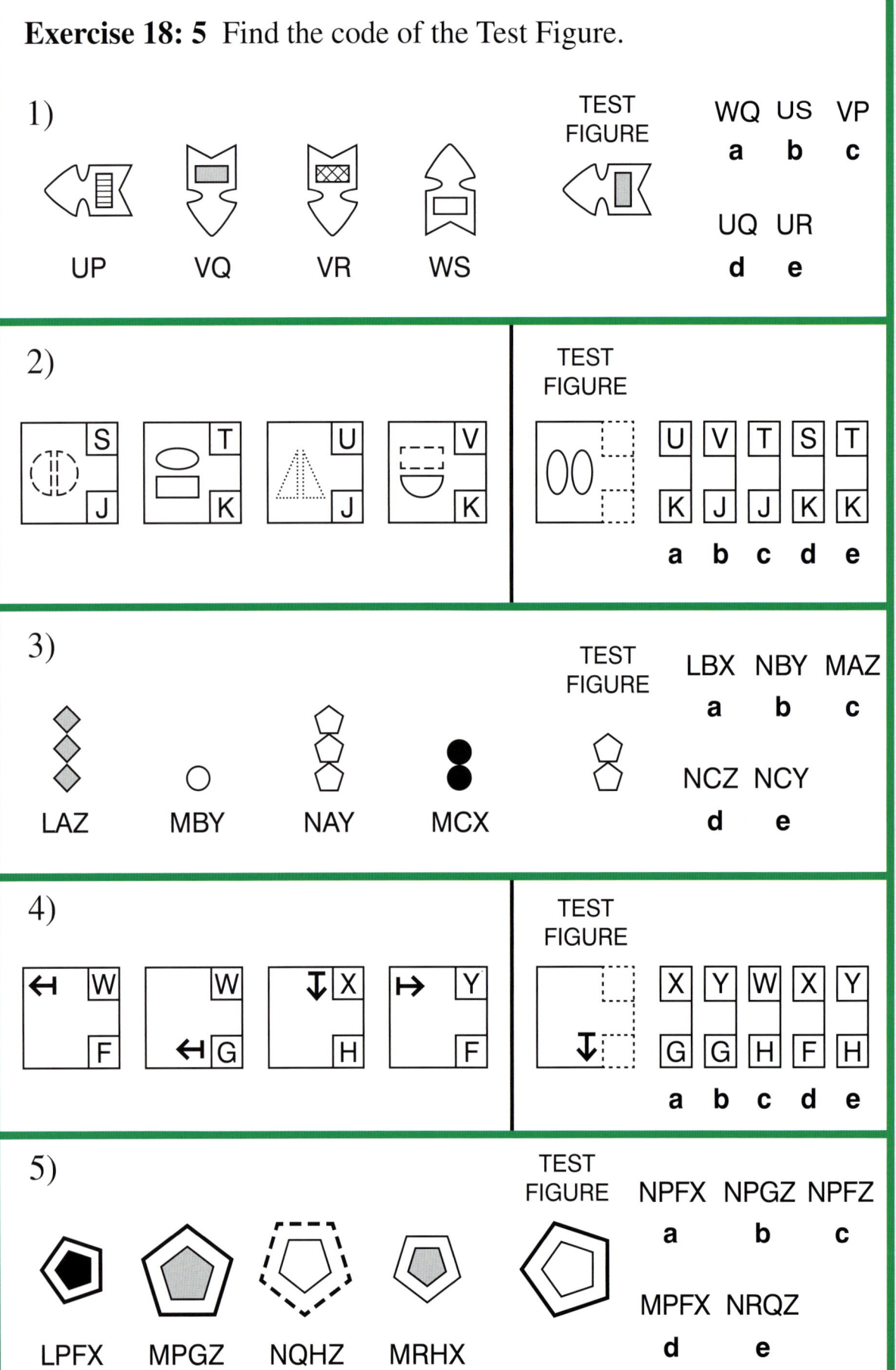

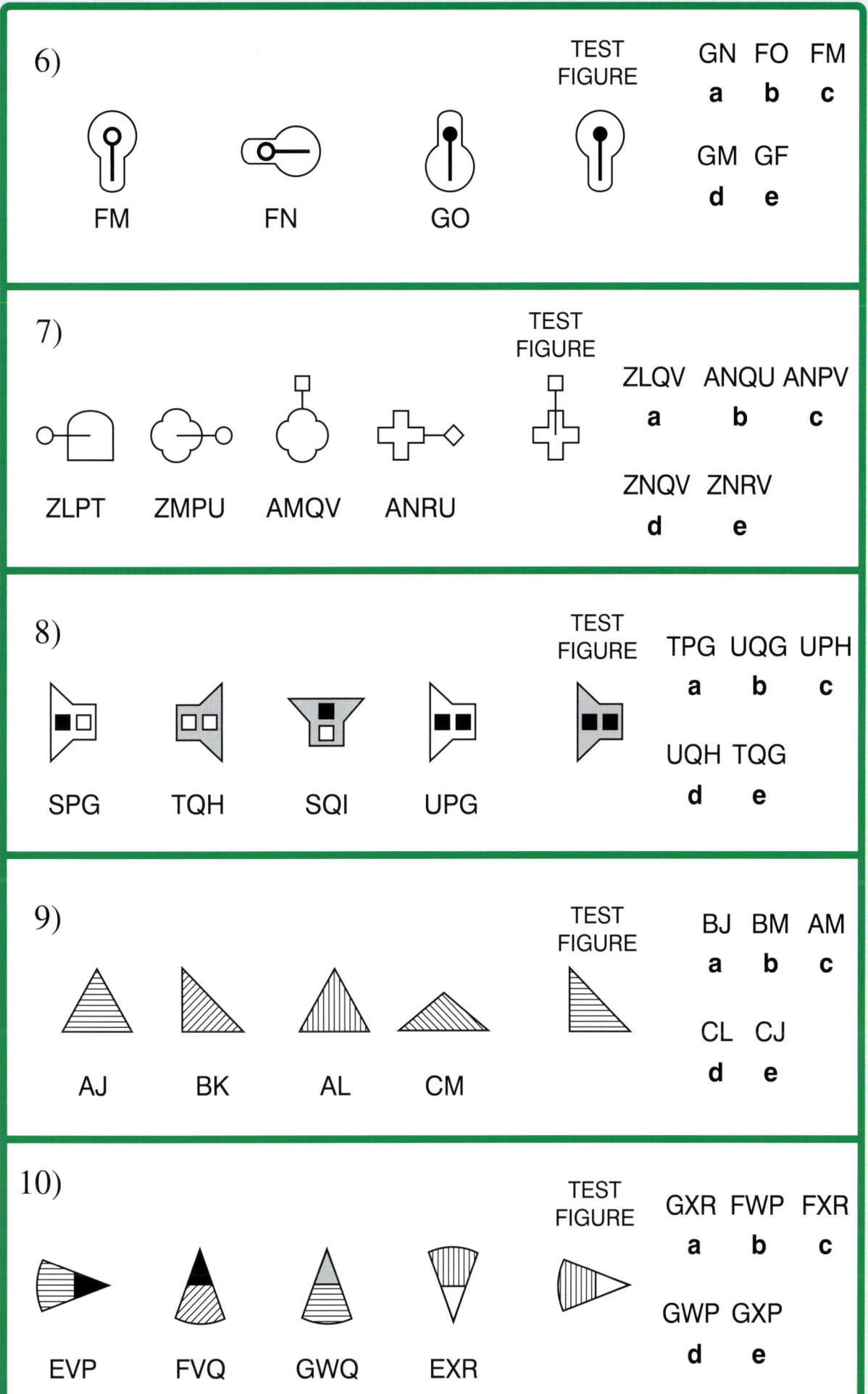

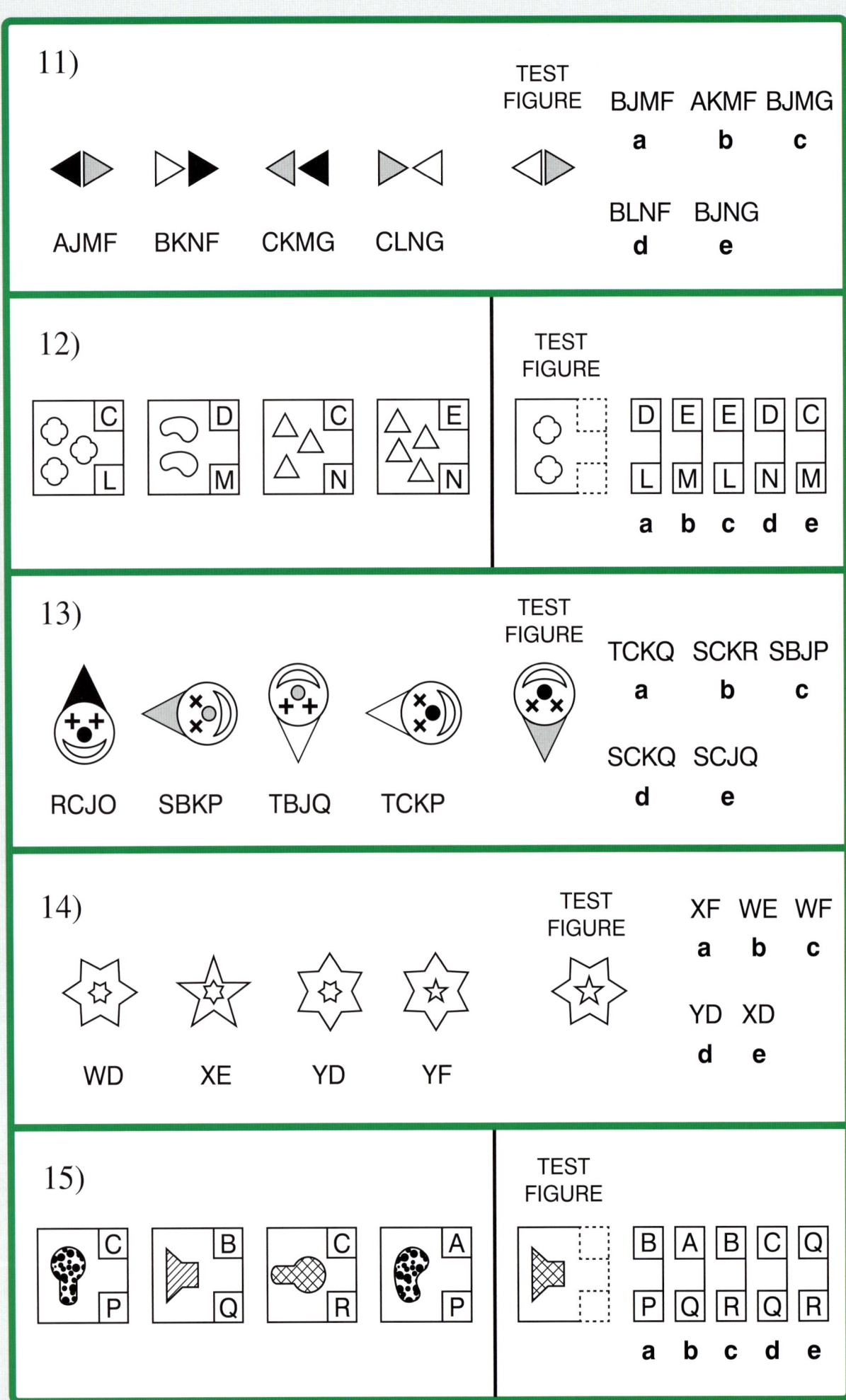

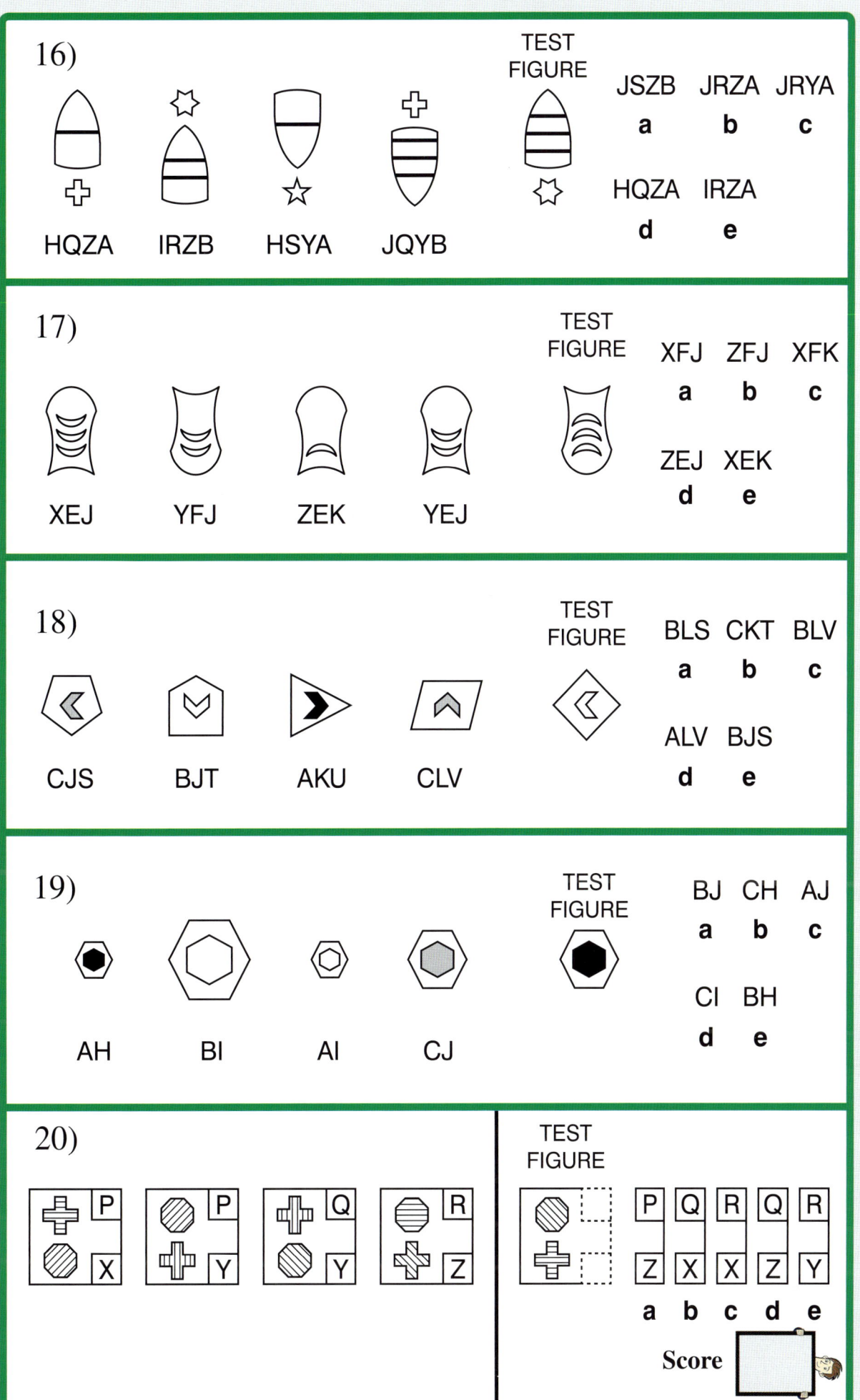

Chapter Nineteen
ANALOGIES
1. Level One

On the left there are two figures with an arrow between them. Decide how the second figure is related to the first. Decide which of the five figures to the right of the arrow goes with the **third** figure to **make a pair** like the two figures on the left.

Example

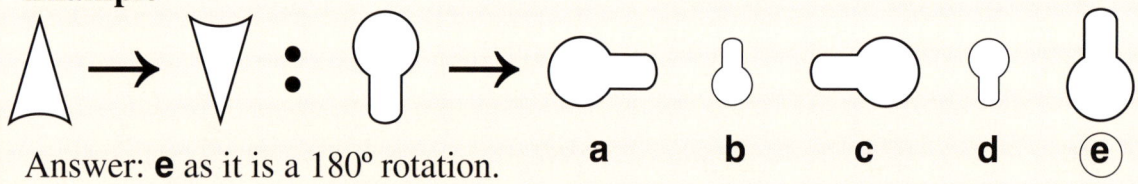

Answer: **e** as it is a 180° rotation.

Exercise 19: 1 Which figure completes the analogy?

1)

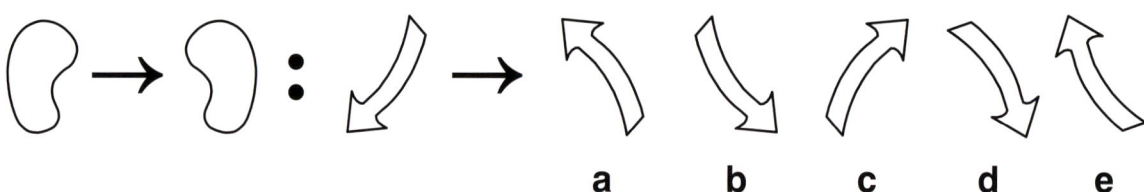

2)

3)

4)

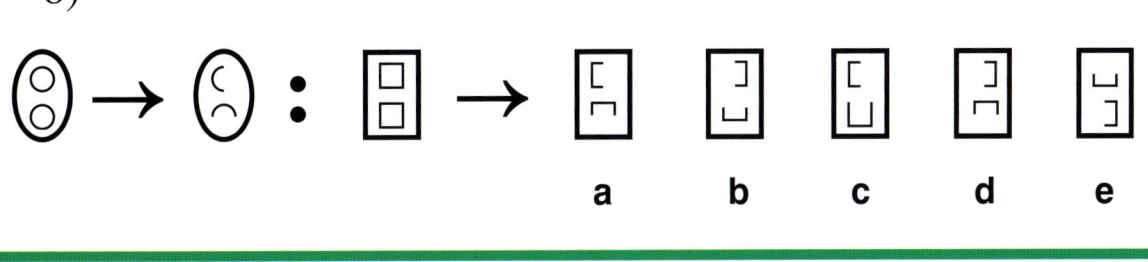
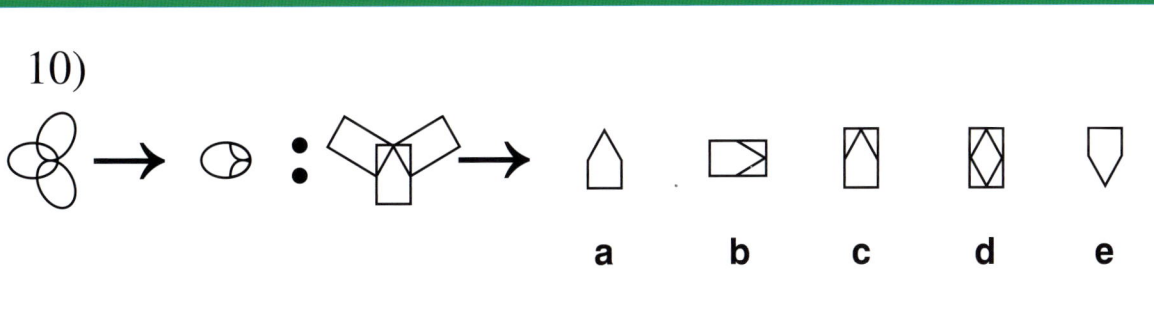

11)

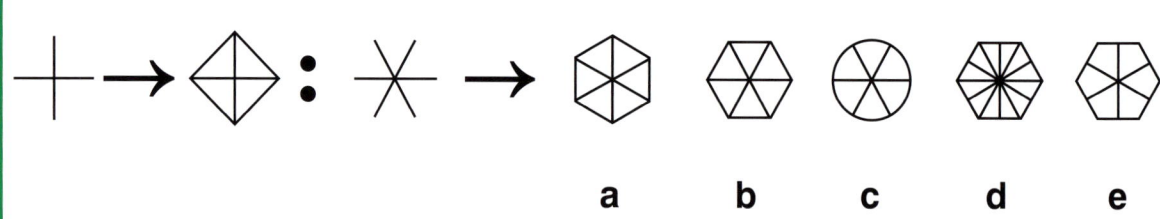

12)

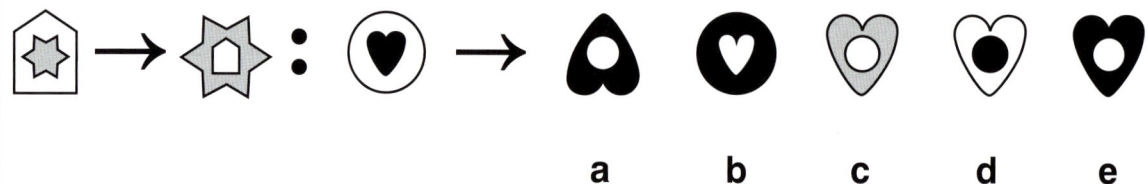

13)

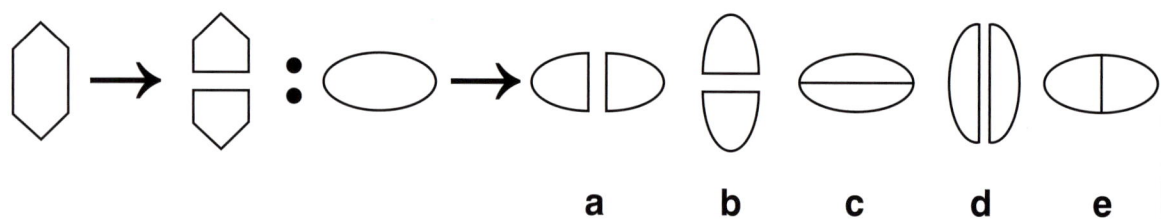

14)

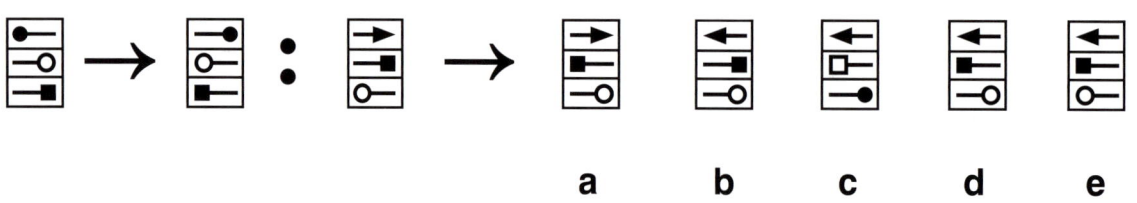

15)

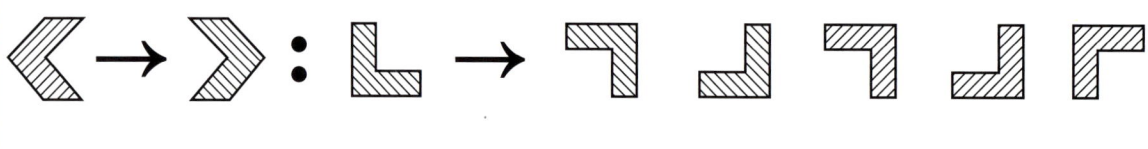

16)

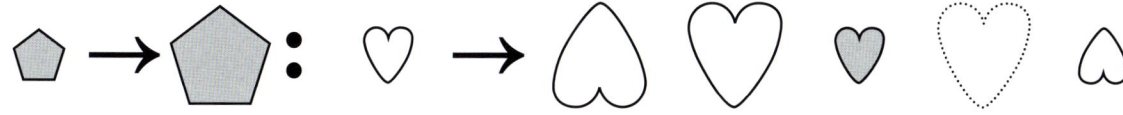

a b c d e

17)

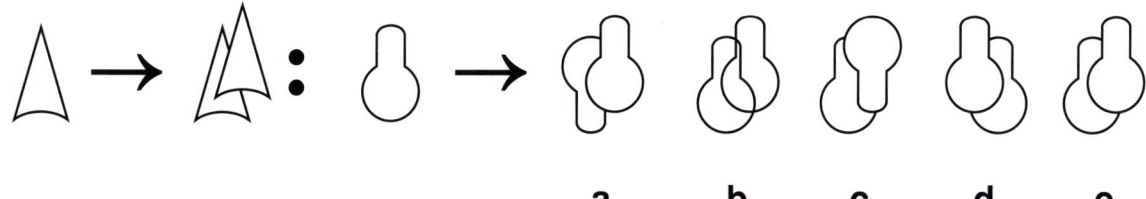

a b c d e

18)

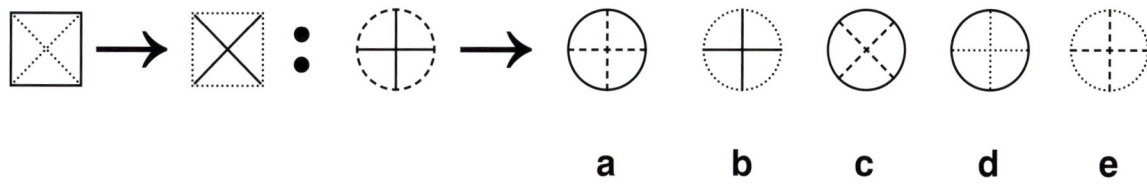

a b c d e

19)

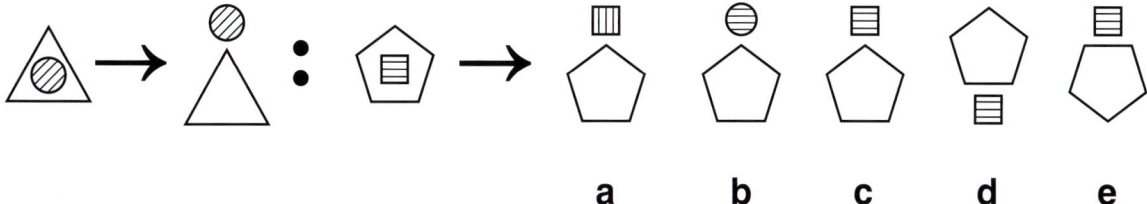

a b c d e

20)

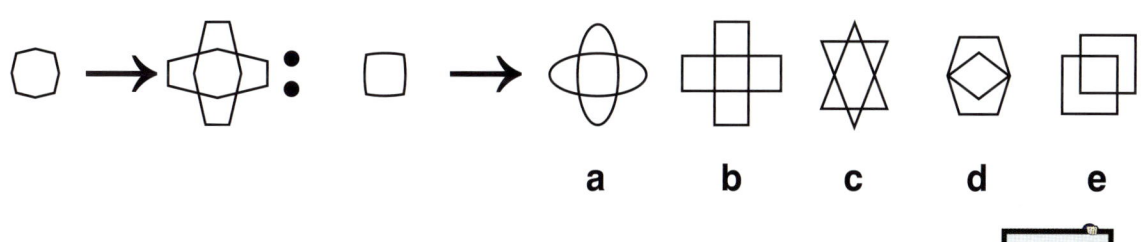

a b c d e

Score

2. Level Two

On the left there are two figures with an arrow between them. Decide how the second figure is related to the first. Decide which of the five figures to the right of the arrow goes with the **third** figure to **make a pair** like the two figures on the left.

Example

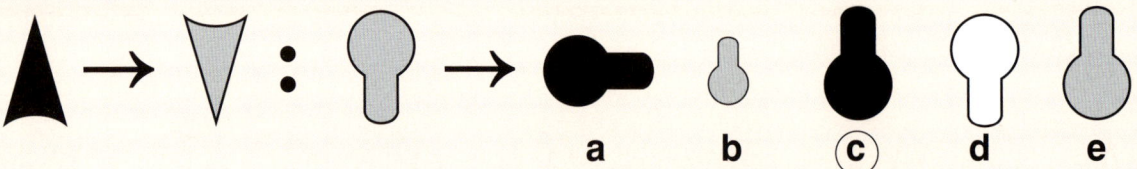

Answer: **c** as it is a 180° rotation and the shading has been reversed.

Exercise 19: 2 Which figure completes the analogy?

1)

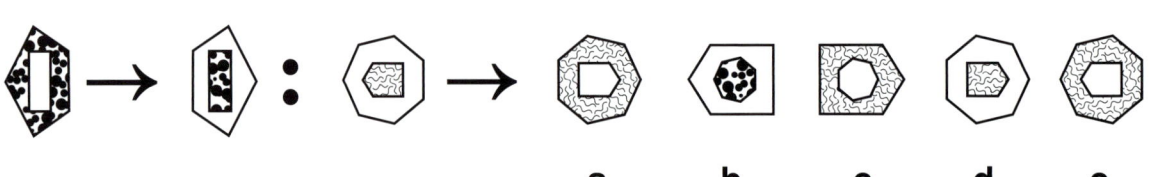

2)

3)

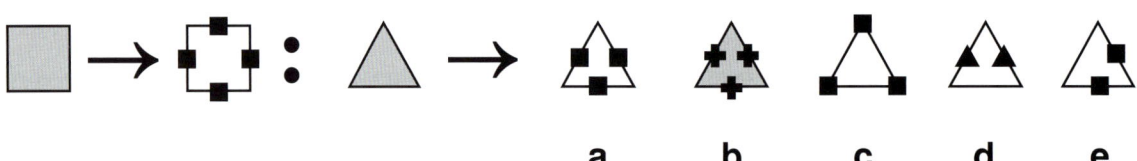

4)

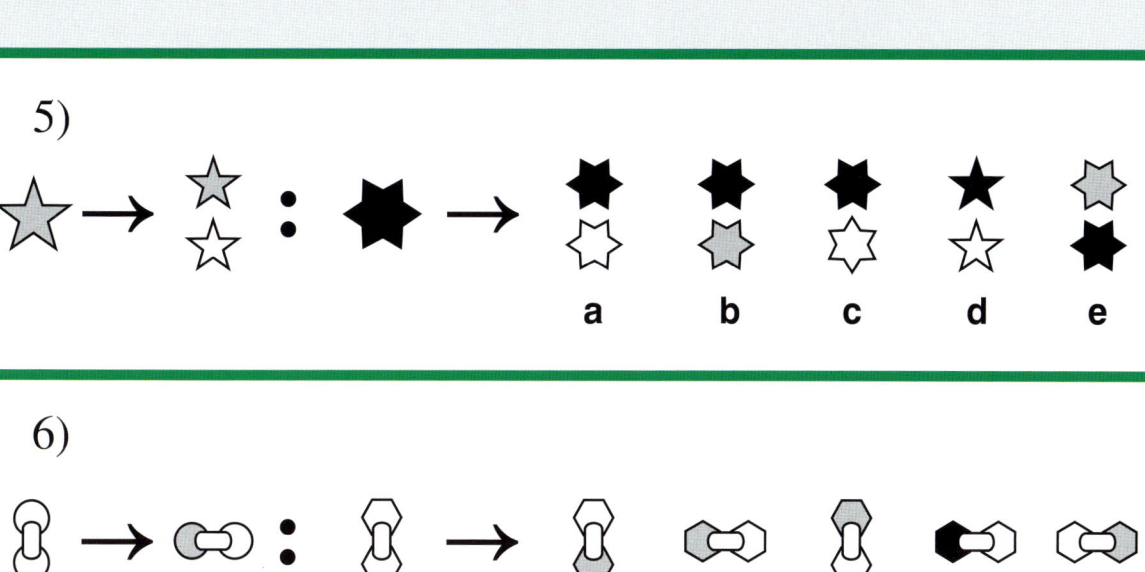
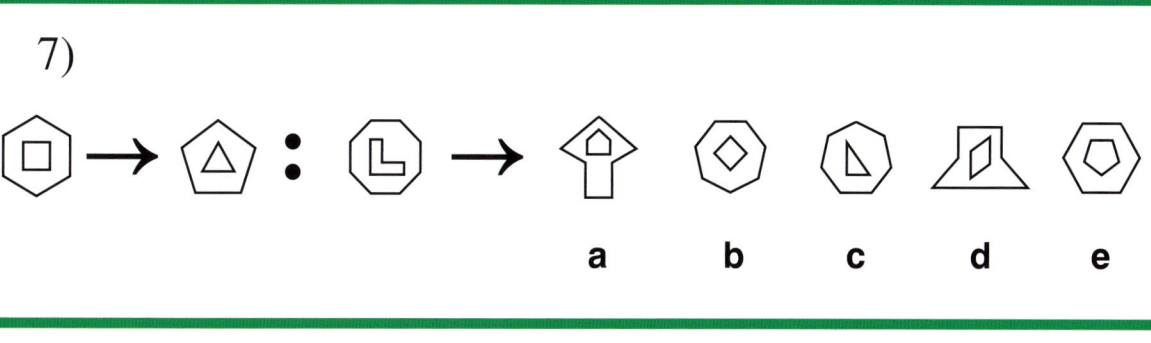
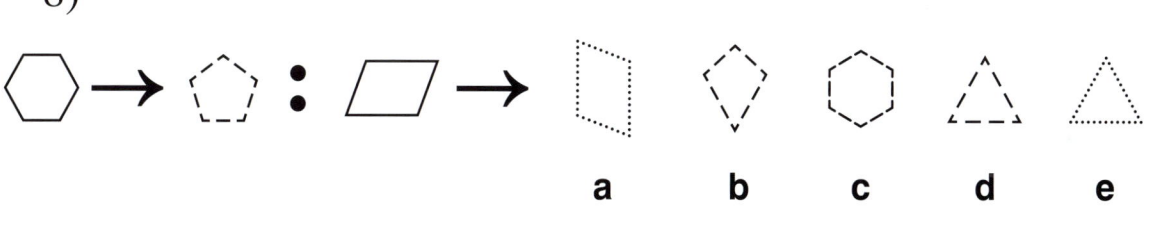
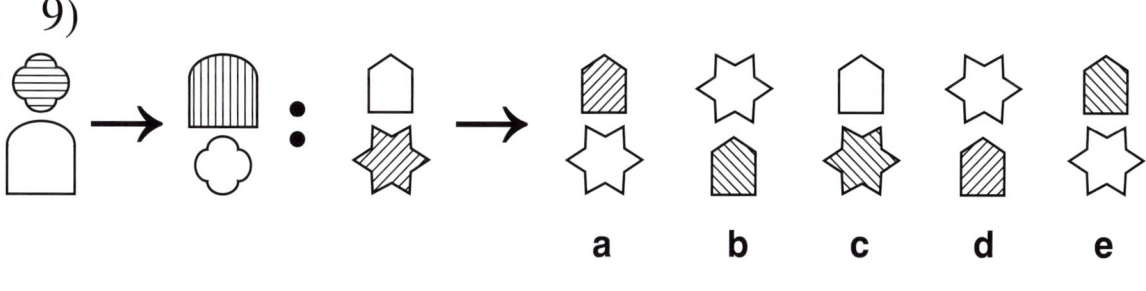
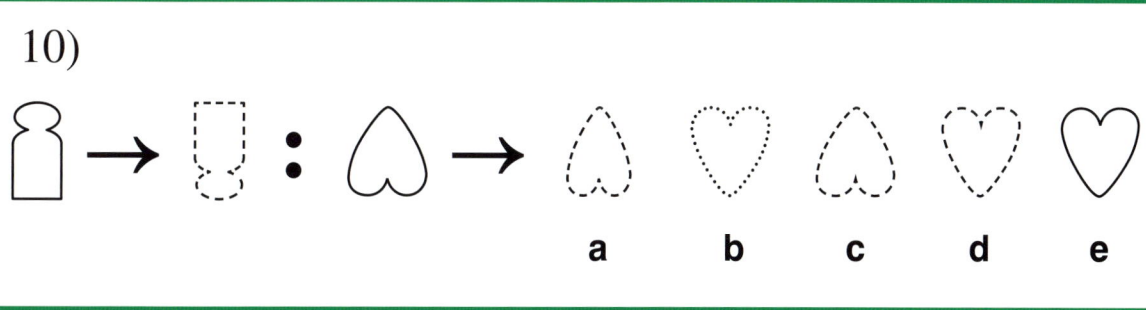

11)

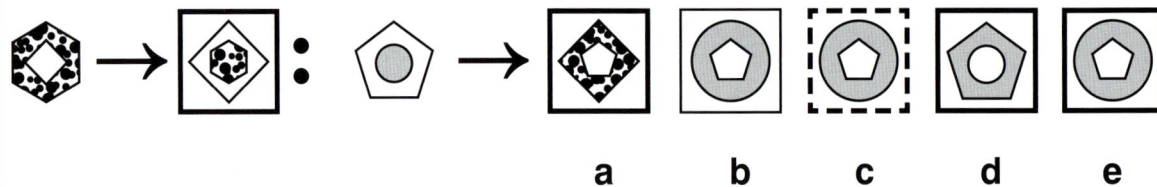

a b c d e

12)

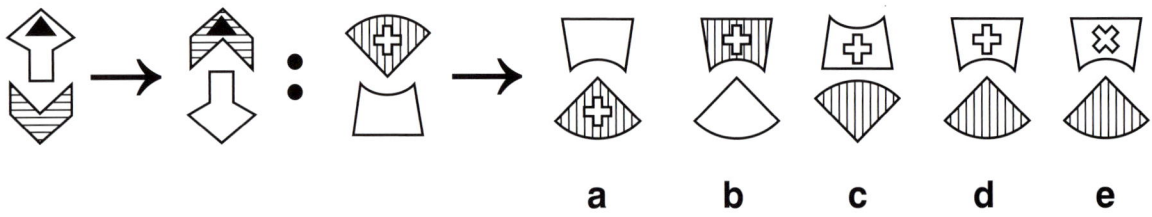

a b c d e

13)

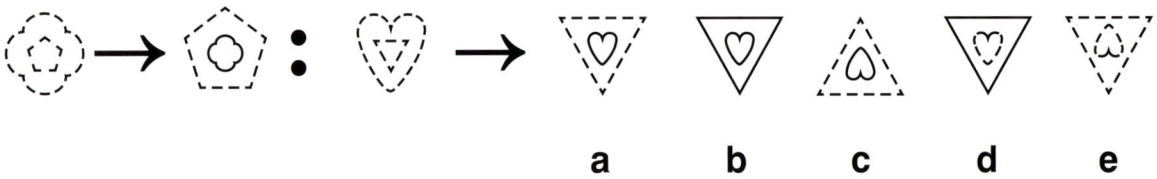

a b c d e

14)

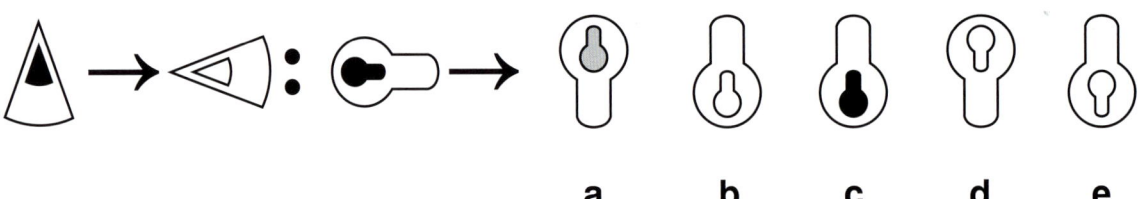

a b c d e

15)

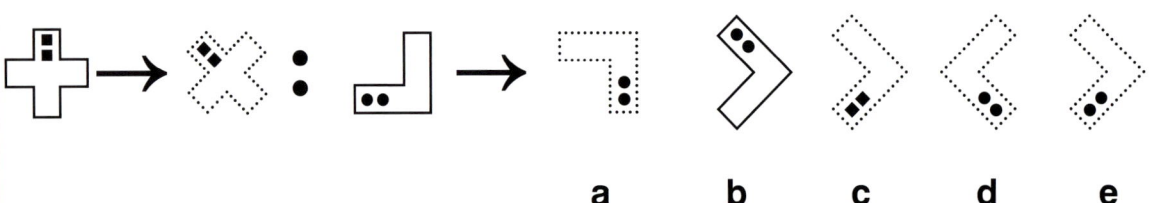

a b c d e

16)

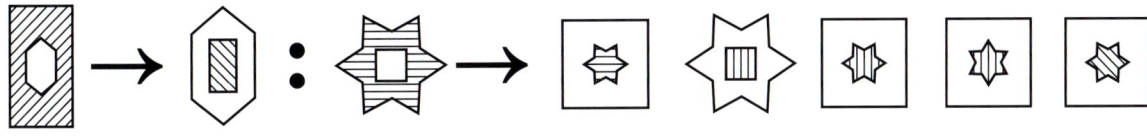

17)

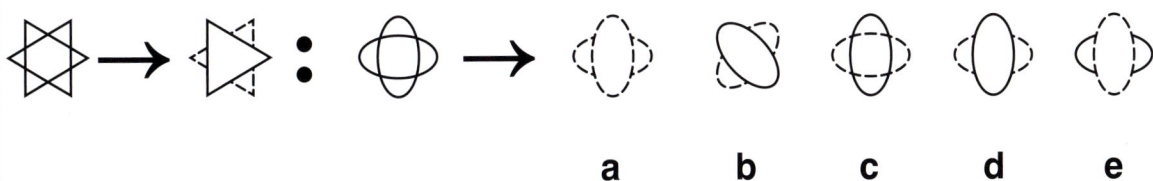

18)

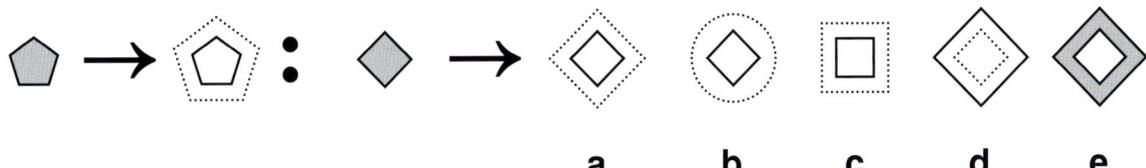

19)

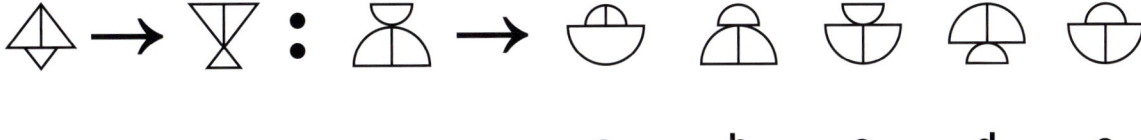

20)

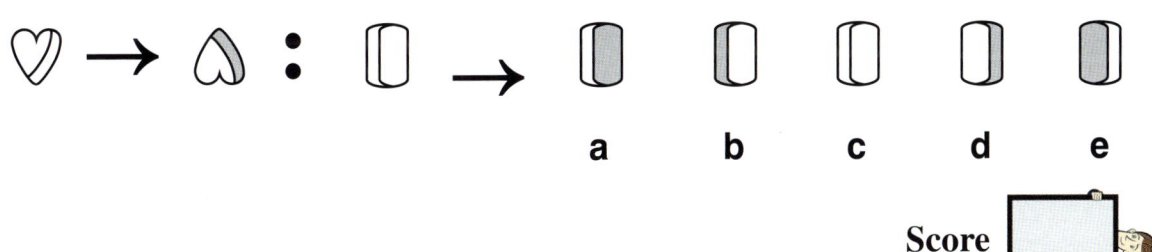

Score

3. Level Three

On the left there are two figures with an arrow between them. Decide how the second figure is related to the first. Decide which of the five figures to the right of the arrow goes with the **third** figure to **make a pair** like the two figures on the left.

Example

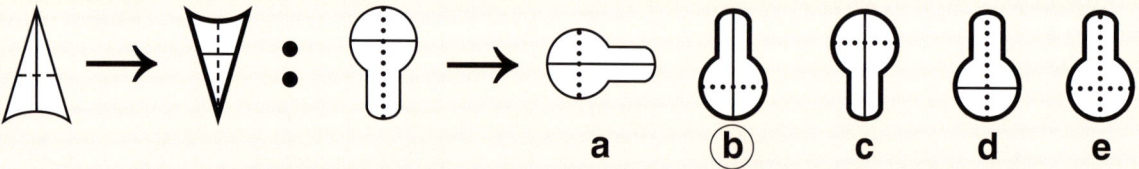

Answer: **b** as it is a 180° rotation, the lines have been reversed and the shape has a Thick Solid Line.

Exercise 19: 3 Which figure completes the analogy?

1)

2)

3)

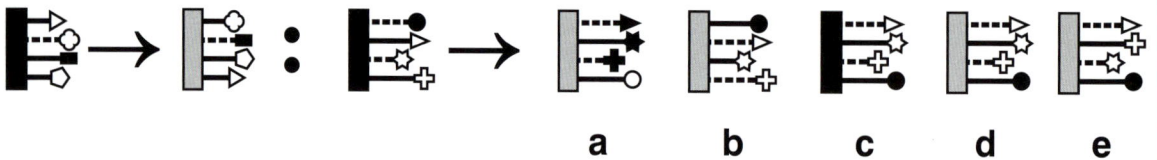

4)

52 © 2011 Stephen Curran

5)
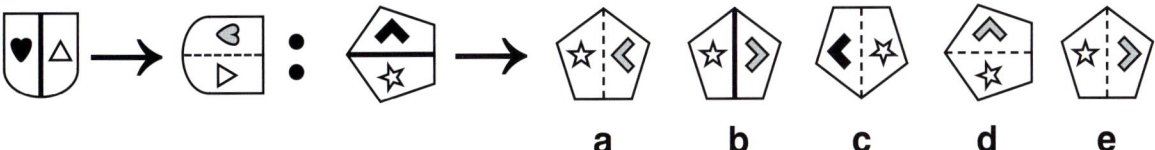

6)
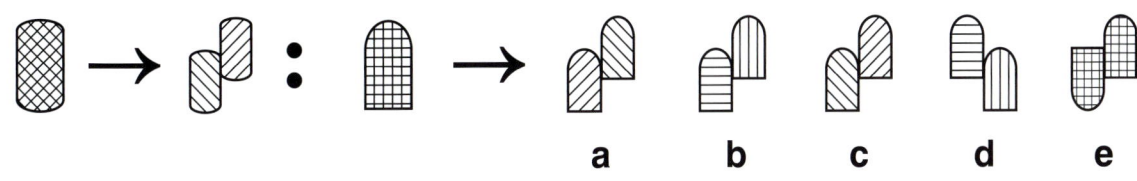

7)
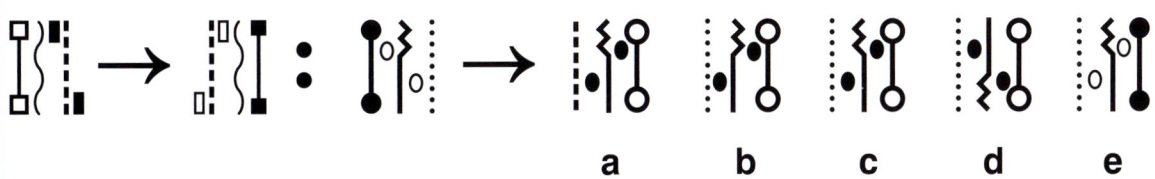

8)
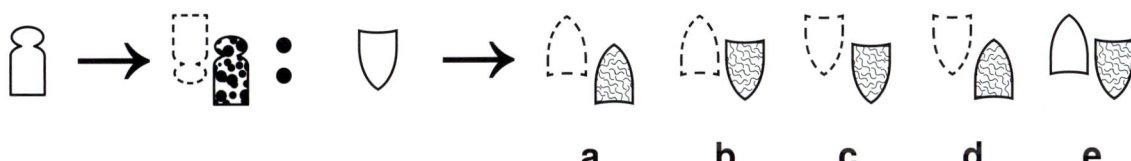

9)
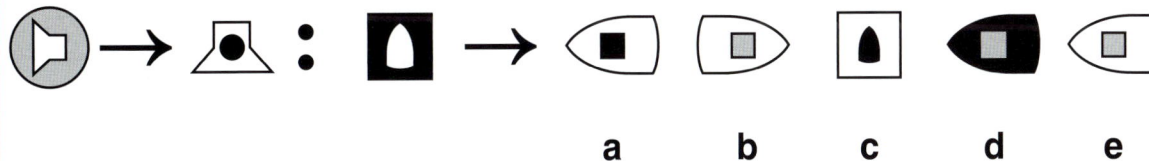

10)
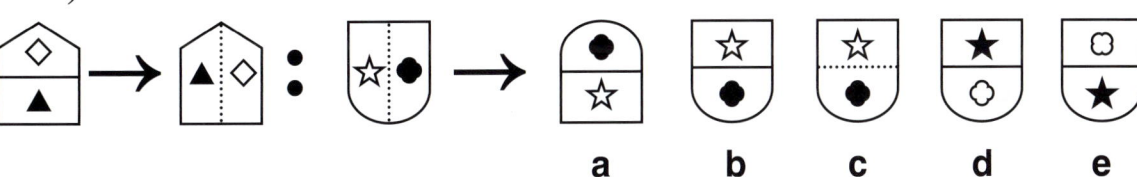

11)

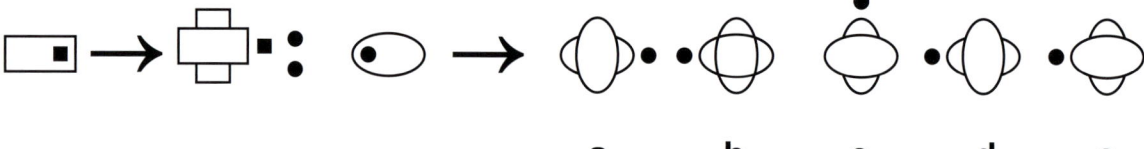

a b c d e

12)

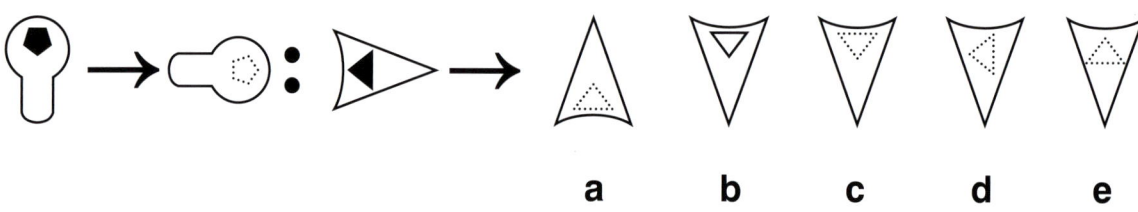

a b c d e

13)

a b c d e

14)

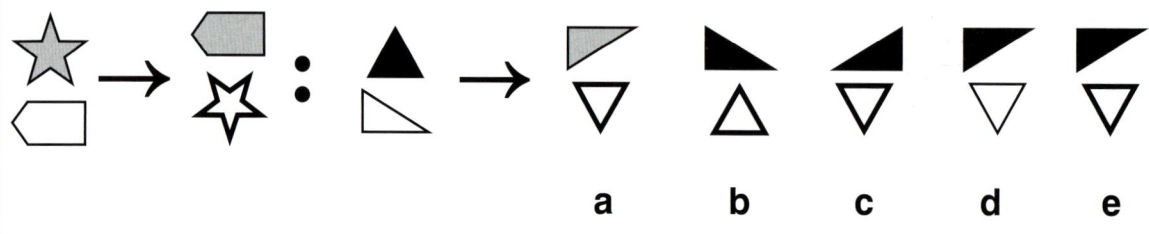

a b c d e

15)

a b c d e

16)

a b c d e

17)

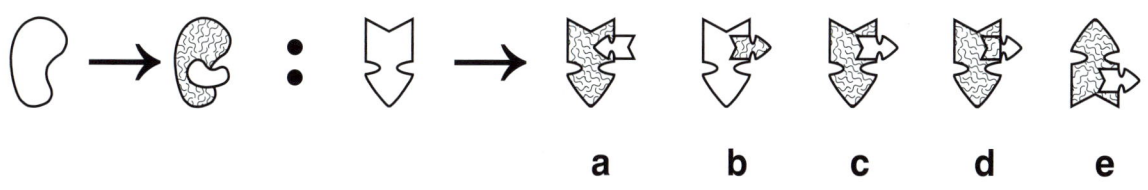

a b c d e

18)

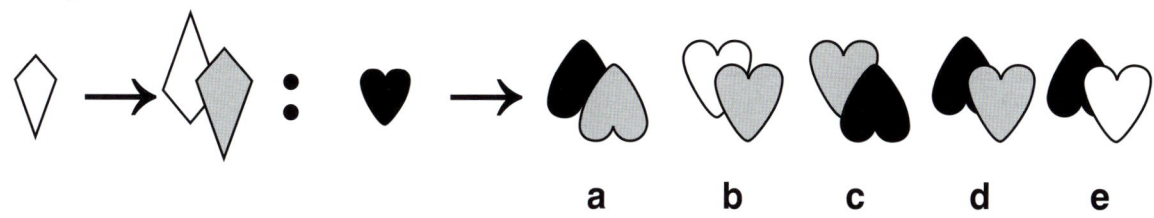

a b c d e

19)

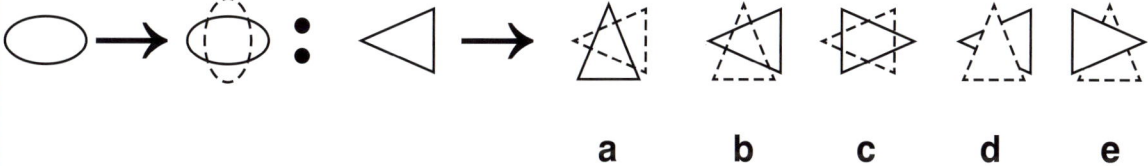

a b c d e

20)

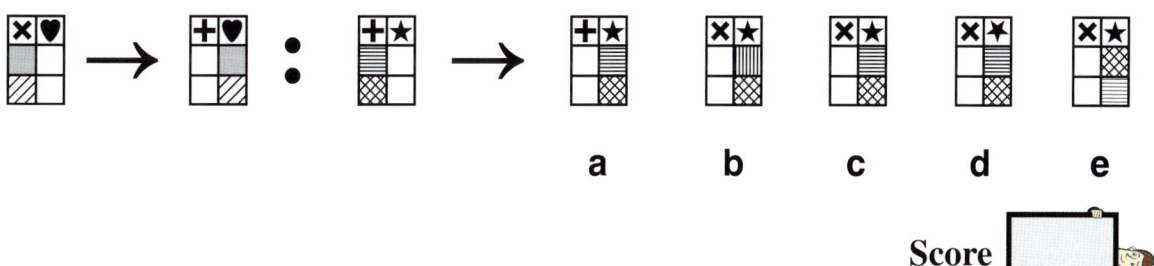

a b c d e

Score

4. Levels Four & Five

On the left are two figures with an arrow between them. Decide how the second figure is related to the first. Decide which of the five figures to the right of the arrow goes with the **third** figure to **make a pair** like the two figures on the left.

Example

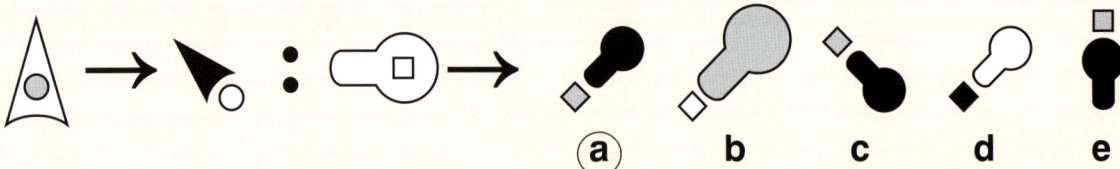

Answer: **a** as it is a 45° anticlockwise rotation, the shapes have been reduced in size, the fills of both shapes have been reversed and the square is no longer enclosed.

Exercise 19: 4 Which figure completes the analogy?

1)

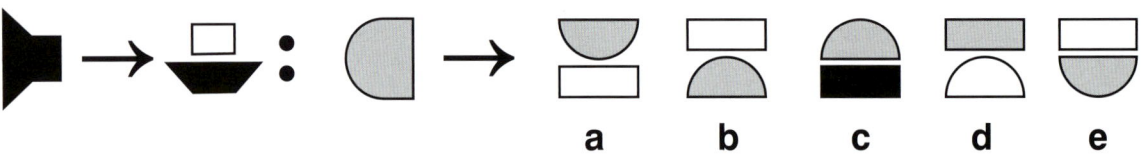

2)

3)

4)

5)

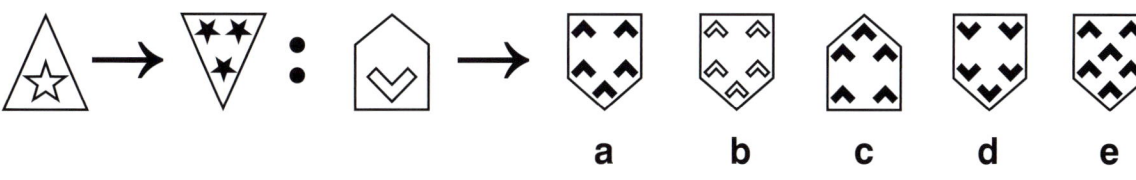

6)

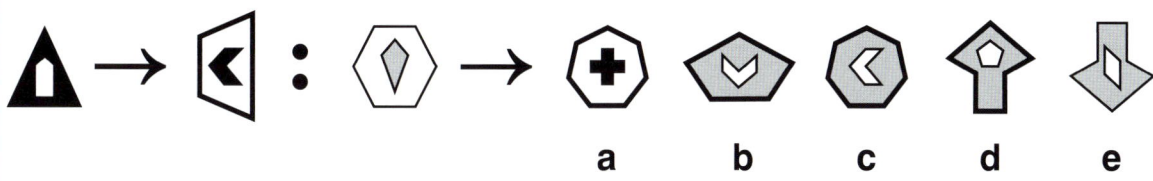

11)

12)

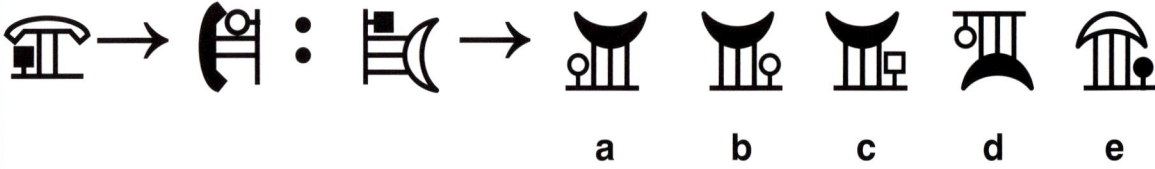

13)

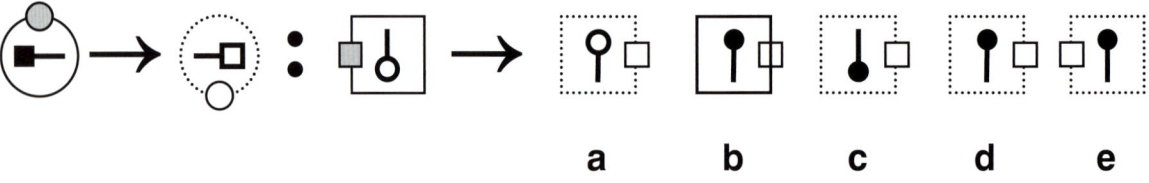

14)

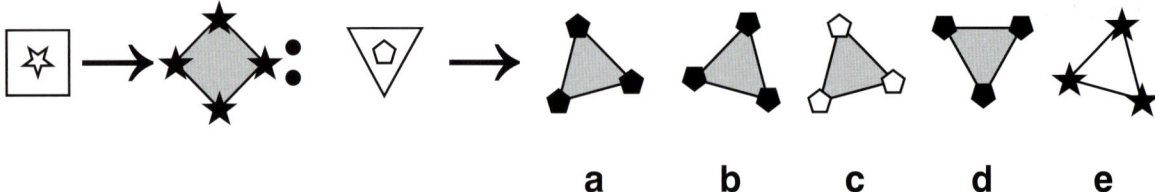

15)

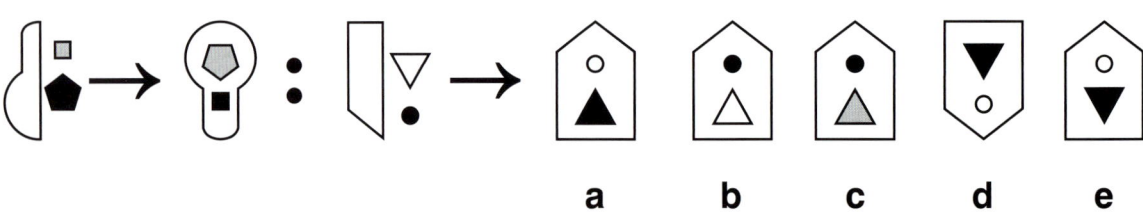

16)
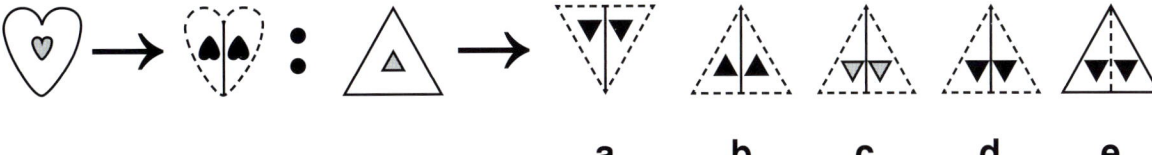

17)
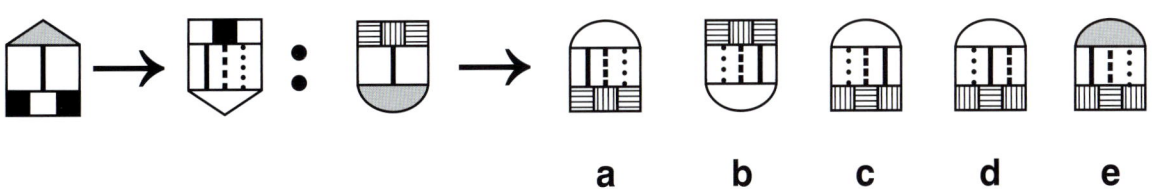

18)
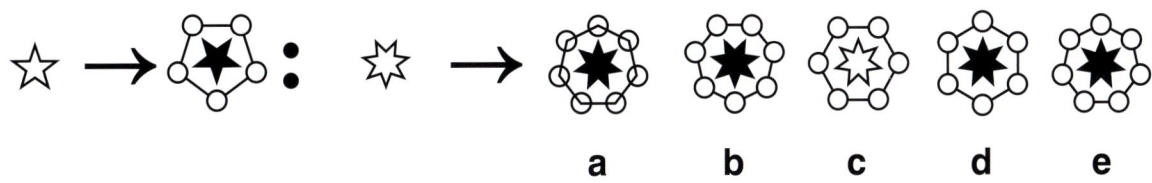

19)
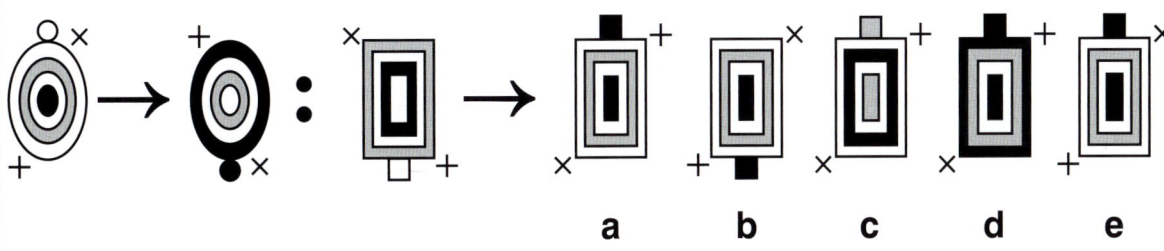

20)
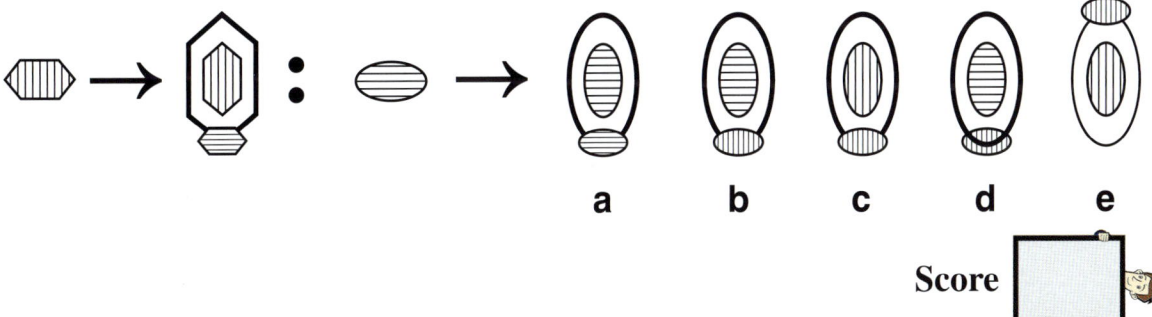

Score

5. Mixed Levels

Exercise 19: 5 Which figure completes the analogy?

1)

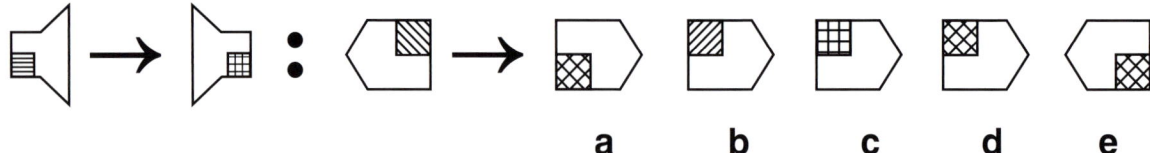

2)

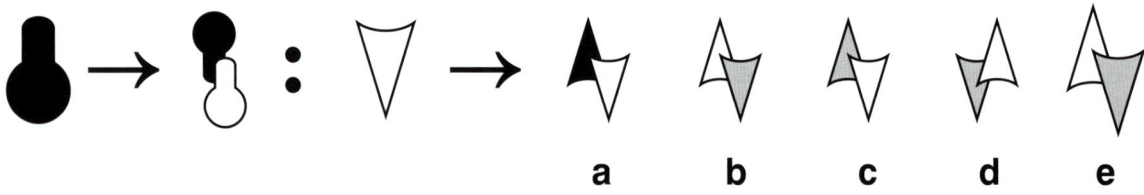

3)

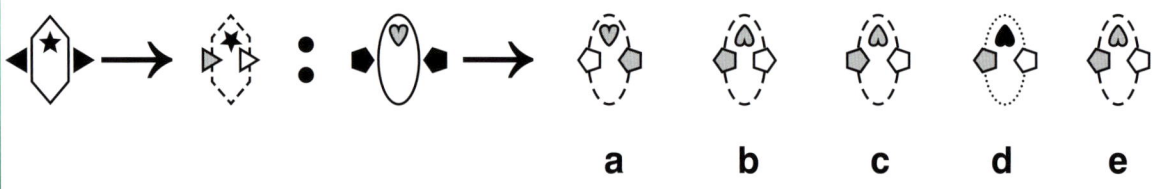

4)

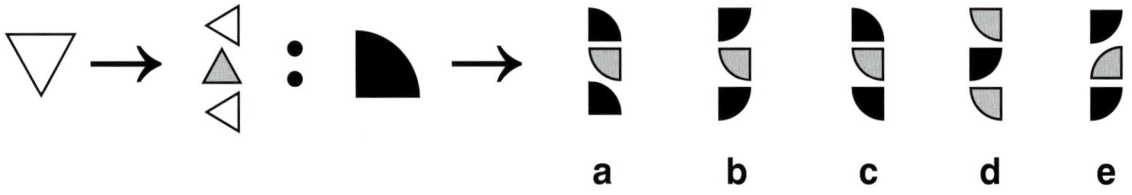

5)

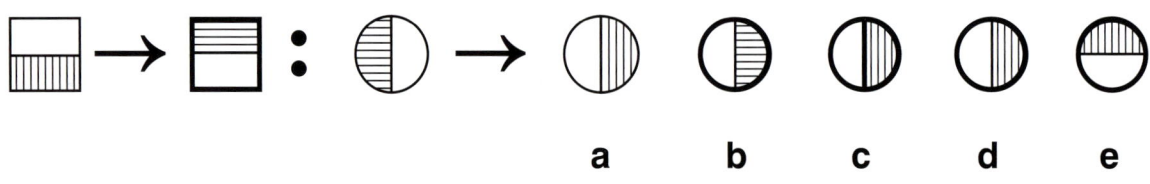

6)

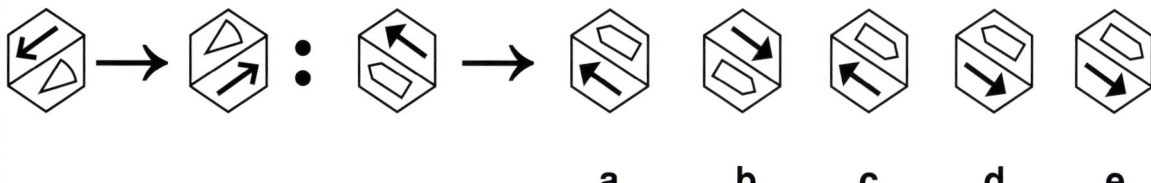

a b c d e

7)

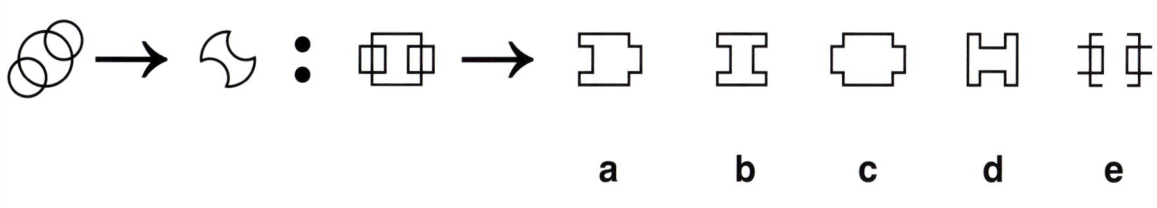

a b c d e

8)

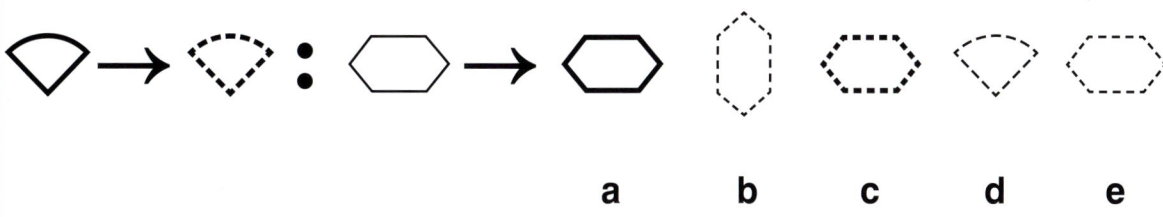

a b c d e

9)

a b c d e

10)

a b c d e

11)

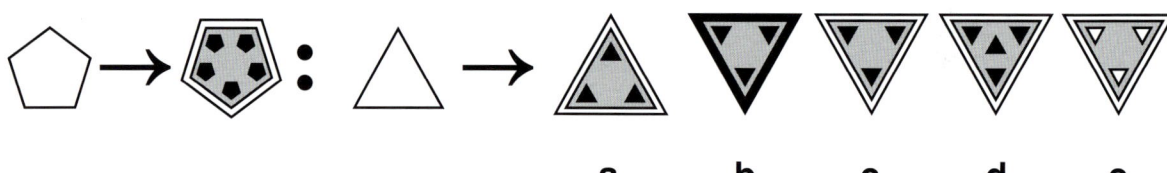

                                                                    a   b   c   d   e

12)

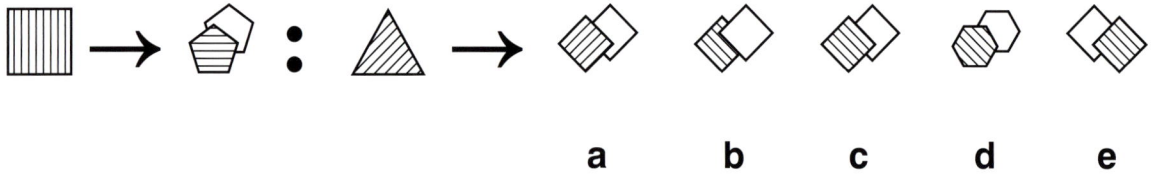

                                                                    a   b   c   d   e

13)

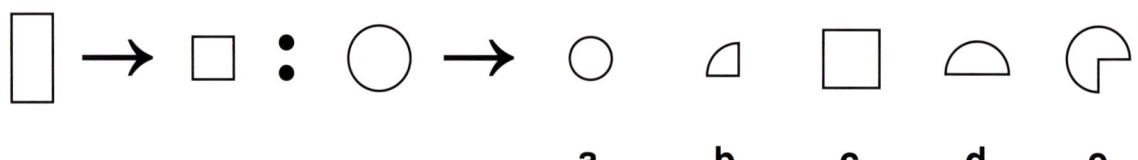

                                                                    a   b   c   d   e

14)

                                                                    a   b   c   d   e

15)

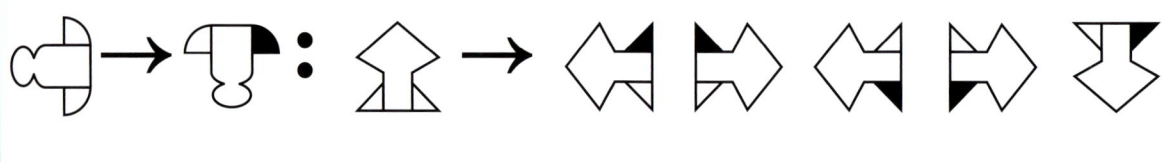

                                                                    a   b   c   d   e

16)
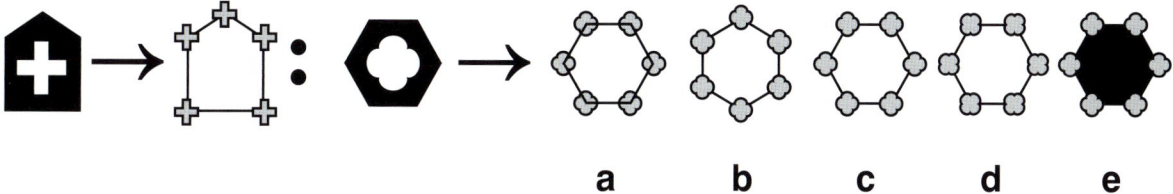

17)
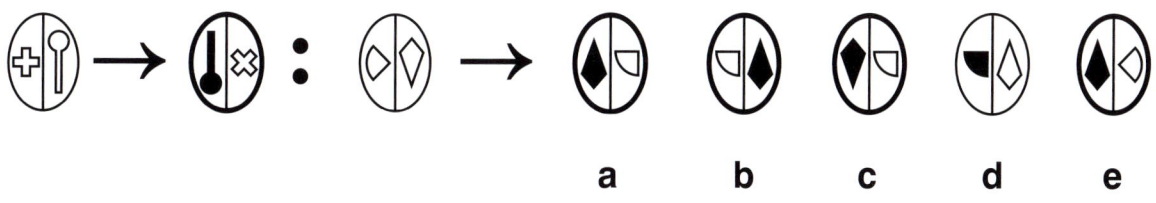

18)
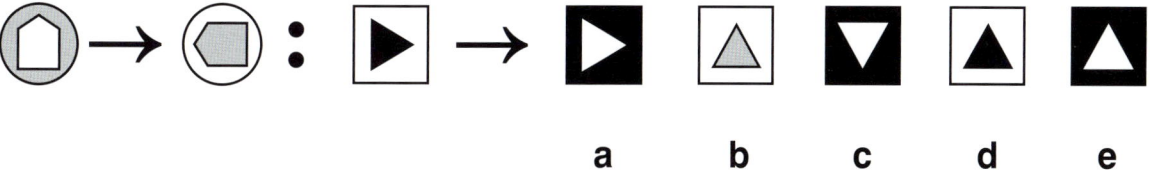

19)
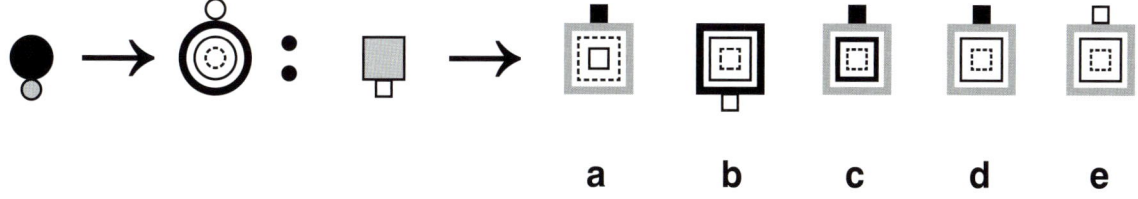

20)
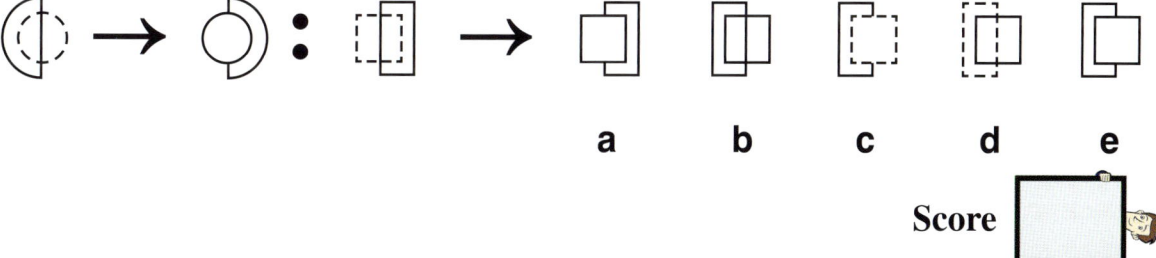

Score

© 2011 Stephen Curran

Answers

*11+ Non-verbal Reasoning
Year 5-7 Workbook 4*

Chapter Seventeen
Odd One Out
Exercise 17: 1
1) **d** - The Circle is not enclosed on the left of the Semi-circle.
2) **b** - The two shapes are not perpendicular to each other.
3) **c** - The figure is not the same rotation as the other figures.
4) **e** - The fill is not Left Slant Shaded.
5) **b** - The diagonal fill is not Right Slant Shaded Fill.
6) **c** - The shape does not have four sides.
7) **a** - The shape does not have a Grey or Black Fill.
8) **b** - The two shapes in the figure are not the same.
9) **a** - The fill is not Left Slant Shaded.
10) **c** - The middle shape is not overlaying the outer shape with a Solid Outline.
11) **e** - The Arrow does not have the same slant as the other Arrows.
12) **d** - The Arrow does not point clockwise.
13) **e** - There are not two vertical H shapes.
14) **a** - The shape does not have a Shaded Fill.
15) **a** - The figure does not have only one Arrowhead.
16) **c** - The two shapes in the figure are not the same.
17) **b** - The two shapes in the figure are not the same.
18) **e** - The Lines do not meet in the centre of the Circle.
19) **c** - The enclosed shape is not an overlay.
20) **b** - The figure does not have only one line of symmetry.

Exercise 17: 2
1) **a** - The number of Crosses is not equal to one more than the number of sides of the shape.
2) **a** - The figure does not contain three long Lines and one short Line.
3) **b** - The two shapes do not face in opposite directions.
4) **e** - The smaller Rectangle does not have a White Fill.
5) **b** - The order of outlines is not Thick, Thin, Thick.
6) **e** - The number of enclosed Circles is not equal to the number of sides of the outer shape.
7) **b** - The Arrow is not pointing upwards.
8) **d** - The Circle with a Grey Fill is not overlaying one of the Circles with a White Fill.
9) **e** - The enclosed Square is not the same rotation as in the other figures.
10) **b** - When positioned vertically, the shape does not have a Vertical Shaded Fill.
11) **e** - The figure does not contain three Squares and two Crosses.
12) **b** - The figure does not include a shape with a Dashed Outline.
13) **e** - The enclosed Line is not a line of symmetry.
14) **e** - The Circle with a Black Fill is not on its own.
15) **a** - The shape does not have an odd number of sides.
16) **d** - The shape is not a rotation of the other shapes.
17) **b** - When rotated so the Arrow is pointing upwards, the Arrow is not on the left of any vertical Ellipses and on the right of any horizontal Ellipses.
18) **c** - The number of sides is increased by 1, not 2.
19) **c** - The Triangles enclosed in the linkage do not have a White Fill.
20) **b** - The shape on the right of the figure is not a reflection of the shape on the left.

Exercise 17: 3
1) **c** - The enclosed shape is not a different rotation to the outer shape.
2) **e** - The Shaded Fill is not Vertical or Diagonal.
3) **b** - The Arrowhead is not open.
4) **e** - The large shape does not have five sides.
5) **b** - The outer shape of the figure is not a rotation of the other figures.

11+ Non-verbal Reasoning Year 5-7 Workbook 4

Answers

6) **c** - There is not only one point between the two Squares.
7) **c** - The small shape with a Black Fill is not with the large shape with a Lattice Fill.
8) **c** - The Arrowhead is not closed.
9) **a** - The number of enclosed Circles does not equal the number of sides of the outer shape.
10) **b** - The fill of the enclosed linkages is not the same.
11) **d** - There are not more Heart Shapes with a White Fill than with a Black Fill.
12) **c** - One of the Squares does not have the same fill as the enclosed Triangle. The Square with the White Fill is not on the left.
13) **a** - The Triangles with Grey and White Fills are not the same rotation as in the other figures.
14) **e** - The Circle is not outside of the shape.
15) **e** - The two shapes do not face in opposite directions.
16) **b** - The Grey Fill is not on the outer sections.
17) **d** - The Ellipse does not have a White or Black Fill.
18) **c** - The Line with a White Circle ending is not long.
19) **b** - The number of Lines is not equal to the number of shapes on each Line.
20) **d** - The number of sides does not total eight.

Exercise 17: 4
1) **a** - The Circle does not enclose three shapes.
2) **d** - The figure does not have a Black Fill.
3) **b** - The line across the middle of the shape is not a line of symmetry.
4) **d** - The Sector does not point clockwise.
5) **c** - The Circle outside the Triangle is not on the edge of the Triangle.
6) **b** - The Lines are not Thick.
7) **a** - The Circle is not on a point.
8) **c** - The Star does not face upwards.
9) **e** - The Arrow does not point between the Circle and the Square.
10) **b** - The figure does not have a Black Fill.
11) **b** - The number of sides of the enclosed shape is not one more than the number of sides of the outer shape.
12) **c** - The Wizard's Hat Shape does not point to the large section of the Triangle.
13) **a** - The number of shapes with a Black Fill is not the same as the number of sides of the shapes.
14) **e** - The outer shape does not have a line of symmetry.
15) **d** - The figure does not have two different fills.
16) **a** - The enclosed Flower Shape is not a different rotation to the outer Flower Shape.
17) **c** - The Circle is not enclosed in the larger section of the Bean Shape.
18) **d** - The Shaded Fill is not Vertical or Horizontal.
19) **b** - The Triangle is not the same rotation as the others.
20) **c** - The number of Circles is not one less than the number of sides of the other shape.

Exercise 17: 5
1) **b** - The number of Moon Shapes is not equal to the number of Shield Shapes.
2) **c** - There is no Circle with a Black Fill.
3) **e** - The large shape does not overlay one of the small shapes.
4) **c** - The enclosed shapes do not have a different orientation from the shapes outside the larger shape.
5) **e** - The Circle with the Black Fill is not on the left.
6) **d** - The figure does not have five sections.
7) **e** - The enclosed shapes are not the same as the outer shape.
8) **a** - The small Moon Shape does not have a White Fill.
9) **c** - The Shaded Fill is not Vertical or Horizontal.
10) **a** - The Horizontal Line is not Thick.
11) **e** - The shape with a Black Fill is not a different rotation to the outer shape.

Answers

11+ Non-verbal Reasoning Year 5-7 Workbook 4

12) **a** - The figure does not have a line of symmetry.
13) **e** - The figure is not a rotation of the other figures.
14) **d** - The Circles do not have a Black or White Fill.
15) **b** - The General Quadrilateral is not the same rotation as the others.
16) **a** - The enclosed Lines do not join two inner points.
17) **d** - The figure does not have a Curved shape.
18) **a** - The figure does not consist of Straight-edged shapes.
19) **e** - The Star does not have a Grey or Black Fill.
20) **d** - When the figures are rotated to the same orientation, the Rectangles do not have the same fill as those in the other figures.

Chapter Eighteen
Codes
Exercise 18: 1
1) **e** - H - Square; Q - Black Fill
2) **b** - T - Solid Outline; G - Rotation of Trapezium
3) **d** - A - Solid Outline; Y - Pentagon
4) **e** - C - Churn Shape points left; N - Large figure
5) **c** - A - Parallelogram; V - Grey Fill
6) **a** - S - Pentagon points upwards; K - Two shapes
7) **b** - Y - Quadrant; O - Dashed Outline
8) **d** - F - Horizontal figure; B - One linkage, one overlay
9) **d** - K - One Bone Shape enclosed; N - Shield Shape
10) **e** - B - Horizontal Shaded Fill; J - Small Circle enclosed
11) **a** - N - Enclosed line figure; G - House Shape
12) **a** - L - White Fill on the right; C - Circle on base
13) **c** - W - Chevron Shape; A - Grey Fill
14) **c** - P - Triangles have Grey Fill; M - Hexagon has Lattice Fill
15) **b** - B - Medium figure; S - Black Fill
16) **e** - Y - One shape; Q - Circle
17) **c** - A - Pencil Shape points left; S - White Fill
18) **a** - N - Enclosed Bone Shape is vertical; H - Speaker Shape
19) **e** - Z - Star inner shape; J - Star outer shape
20) **c** - V - Star points downwards; F - Thick Outline

Exercise 18: 2
1) **b** - N - Dashed Outline; X - Flower Shape
2) **a** - E - Vertical Shaded Fill; S - Two Circles have Black Fill
3) **a** - T - Pentagon; G - Rotated Cross enclosed
4) **c** - B - Dashed Outline; X - Medium enclosure
5) **a** - H - Small figure; T - Chevron Shape points upwards
6) **d** - N - Arrow points downwards; E - Star positioned in top left corner
7) **c** - B - Cross; X - Grey and White Fills
8) **b** - L - Rotation of Quadrant; P - Quadrant positioned in bottom left corner
9) **e** - L - Triangle and Square; P - Grey and White Fill
10) **e** - L - Curved Arrow points left; Q - Diagonal Shaded Fill
11) **c** - M - Grey Fill; X - Fill in top left quadrant
12) **c** - Q - Helmet Shape; J - Enclosed H Shape
13) **b** - G - Square; S - Enclosed shape has Dotted Outline
14) **a** - B - Figure positioned diagonally; H - Heart Shape positioned at end of Cigar Shape
15) **e** - J - Cross with White Fill enclosed in shape with Black Fill; Y - Both Squares have Grey Fill
16) **a** - E - Both Crosses have White Fill; P - Crosses are positioned vertically on the right

11+ Non-verbal Reasoning
Year 5-7 Workbook 4

Answers

17) **d** - G - Quadrant points upwards;
    R - Bulb Shape points right
18) **c** - M - Pentagon; I - Four shapes
19) **b** - Y - Arrow positioned on the right;
    F - Circle has single Solid Outline
20) **a** - Y - Grey Fill; L - Horizontal Shaded Fill

Exercise 18: 3

1) **a** - X - Large Heart Shape points upwards;
   C - Small Heart Shape on the right;
   H - Small Heart Shape points upwards
2) **d** - P - Circle; B - Solid Outline; V - Left Slant Shaded Fill
3) **c** - K - Orientation of Bean Shape;
   B - Horizontal Line Fill if Bean Shape is positioned vertically; T - Enclosed Circle has White Fill
4) **b** - Y - Large Ellipse; E - Large Rectangle;
   V - Grey Fill
5) **e** - Q - Large figure; X - Thick Outline;
   L - White Fill
6) **d** - H - Two Lines; T - Stretched Cigar Shape; M - Vertical Lines
7) **d** - D - Dotted Outline; P - Arrow points left; A - Medium Arrow
8) **c** - R - Star; M - Four enclosed Circles;
   P - White Fill
9) **e** - A - Single Triangle points upwards;
   Y - Single Triangle has White Fill;
   L - One Grey Fill
10) **a** - A - White Fill; L - Pencil Shape;
    Z - Pencil Shape points upwards
11) **e** - S - Square; Q - Black Fill; B - Four sections
12) **c** - T - Black Circle enclosed; G - Helmet Shape points right; C - Cigar Shape enclosed
13) **a** - Q - Rotated Cross; Y - Shield Shape;
    C - House Shape
14) **d** - B - Rotation of General Quadrilateral;
    L - Grey Fill; F - Medium figure
15) **b** - K - Enclosed shape has Grey Fill;
    V - Large shape has Speckled Fill;
    B - Enclosed Star is rotated
16) **e** - O - Horizontal figure; C - Circles;
    U - Four shapes

17) **c** - F - Outer Circle has Black Fill;
    Y - Inner Circle has Horizontal Shaded Fill; P - Middle Circle has White Fill
18) **a** - Z - Enclosed shape has Grey Fill;
    I - Enclosed shape is positioned at bottom right or outer shape; M - Wide Shaded Fill
19) **d** - A - Linkage has Black Fill; T - Figure is diagonal; O - Sectors
20) **e** - R - Semi-circle has Dotted Outline;
    W - Ellipse is enclosed; T - Ellipse has Solid Outline

Exercise 18: 4

1) **e** - S - Arrow has Grey Fill; X - Black Outer Circle; B - Arrow points left;
   L - Enclosed Circle has White Fill
2) **b** - P - Dotted Outline; G - Two enclosed Circles; C - Sea Horse Shape is horizontal; V - Circles have White Fill
3) **e** - M - Solid Outline; E - Enclosed Pentagon has White Fill; R - Large Pentagon points upwards; F - Large Pentagon has Lattice Fill
4) **c** - T - Three Squares; X - Small Squares overlay large Square; A - Dashed Outline;
   L - Enclosed Square with Black Fill
5) **d** - A - Large shape has White Fill;
   Y - Enclosed shape has Black Fill;
   J - Enclosed shape is a Set Square Shape;
   Q - Shield Shape
6) **b** - M - Triangles; E - Point to point horizontally; U - Horizontal reflection;
   B - Grey and White Fills
7) **a** - L - Grey Fill; S - Three Crosses;
   X - Vertical Cross; C - Pencil Shape points upwards
8) **c** - P - Four lines and shapes; F - Grey Fill; D - Decreasing in height; R - Squares
9) **d** - D - Triangle points upwards;
   M - Grey Fill; Z - Enclosed Circle;
   G - Spike Shape points right
10) **a** - D - Horizontal; X - Linkage has Black Fill; Q - Circles; J - Left Slant Shaded Fill
11) **e** - E - Black Fill; X - Dashed Outline;
    M - Heart Shape on top right point of Pentagon; B - Heart Shape points right

Answers

11+ Non-verbal Reasoning Year 5-7 Workbook 4

12) **e** - S - Enclosed Pentagon; X - Enclosed shape has Lattice Fill; F - Circle; B - Large shape has Grey Fill
13) **c** - D - Spike Shape points upwards; K - Enclosed shape has Black Fill; Q - Enclosed Square; Y - No enclosed Line
14) **b** - S - Large enclosed Triangle has Black Fill; B - Small enclosed Triangle has Black Fill; K - Triangle points left; G - One enclosed Line
15) **c** - T - Vertical Figure; C - Black Fill; Z - Circle; L - Two shapes
16) **c** - P - Small Flower Shape; N - Dashed Outline; B - Small shape enclosed in bottom shape; G - Hexagons
17) **e** - F - Thin Solid Outline; R - Enclosed Cross Shape; Z - Two enclosed shapes; V - Quadrant points upwards
18) **a** - B - Circle has Horizontal Shaded Fill; L - Moon Shape at the top; Z - Moon Shape has White Fill; P - Three Circles have Grey Fill
19) **c** - Z - Star Shape; G - Enclosed Phone Shape; O - Enclosed shape has Black Fill; U - Large shape has Grey Fill
20) **b** - R - Enclosed Circles; B - Parallelogram; Z - White Fill; J - Four enclosed shapes

Exercise 18: 5

1) **d** - U - Curved Arrow points left; Q - Grey Fill
2) **c** - T - Solid Outline; J - Same shapes
3) **e** - N - Pentagons; C - Two shapes; Y - White Fill
4) **a** - X - Arrow points downwards; G - Figure in bottom right of square
5) **c** - N - White Fill; P - Thick Outline; F - Pentagon points left; Z - Large figure
6) **d** - G - Line ending has Black Fill; M - Bulb Shape points downwards
7) **d** - Z - Overlay; N - Loaf Shape; Q - Square line ending; V - Line at the top
8) **b** - U - Squares have Black Fill; Q - Speaker Shape has Grey Fill; G - Speaker Shape points left
9) **a** - B - Right-angled Triangle; J - Horizontal Shaded Fill
10) **e** - G - Horizontal Shaded Fill when Sector points downwards; X - Tip has White Fill; P - Sector points right
11) **a** - B - Left Triangle has White Fill; J - Right Triangle has Grey Fill; M - Left Triangle points left; F - Right Triangle points right
12) **a** - D - Two shapes; L - Flower Shapes
13) **d** - S - Wizard's Hat Shape has Grey Fill; C - Small Circle has Black Fill; K - Rotated Crosses; Q - Figure points downwards
14) **c** - W - Outer Shape is horizontal 6-pointed Star Shape; F - Enclosed Shape is 5-pointed Star Shape
15) **c** - B - Speaker Shape; R - Lattice Fill
16) **b** - J - Three enclosed Lines; R - Small shape is 6-pointed Star Shape; Z - Shield Shape points upwards; A - Small shape is under Shield Shape
17) **c** - X - Three enclosed Moon Shapes; F - Helmet Shape points downwards; K - Moon Shapes point downwards
18) **a** - B - White Fill; L - Four-sided outer shape; S - Chevron Shape points left
19) **b** - C - Medium-sized figure; H - Black Fill
20) **b** - Q - Octagon has Left Slant Shaded Fill; X - Cross has Horizontal Shaded Fill

Chapter Nineteen

Analogies

Exercise 19: 1

1) **b** - The shape has been flipped horizontally.
2) **e** - One side has been added to the shape.
3) **a** - The fills have been swapped.
4) **c** - The figure has been rotated 180°.
5) **e** - The Shaded Fill has been rotated 90°.
6) **b** - The fills have been swapped.
7) **d** - The figure has been flipped horizontally.
8) **a** - The right half of the top enclosed shape and the bottom half of the bottom enclosed shape have been subtracted.

11+ Non-verbal Reasoning
Year 5-7 Workbook 4

Answers

9) **c** - The right half of the shape has been subtracted.
10) **c** - The outer shapes have been removed, leaving the middle shape and the linkages.
11) **b** - The ends of the Lines have been connected by Straight Lines to become lines of symmetry.
12) **e** - The shapes have been swapped.
13) **a** - The shape has been split in half and separated out.
14) **d** - The figure has been flipped horizontally.
15) **d** - The figure has been flipped horizontally.
16) **b** - The shape has been enlarged.
17) **e** - A replica of the original shape has been added as an overlay.
18) **a** - The line types have been swapped.
19) **c** - The inner shape has been vertically transposed so the enclosed shape has been moved to above the large shape.
20) **a** - The shape has become the linkage shape of two identical perpendicular shapes.

Exercise 19: 2

1) **e** - The top shape has been enlarged to become the outer shape. The bottom shape has become the enclosure.
2) **a** - The figure has been flipped horizontally. The fills have been swapped.
3) **a** - The Grey Fill has become White. A Square with a Black Fill has been added as an overlay to each side.
4) **c** - The shape has been rotated 90° anticlockwise, then flipped horizontally. The Solid Outline has become Dashed.
5) **a** - The shape has been reduced and become the top shape. A duplicate of the smaller shape with a White Fill has been added below.
6) **b** - The figure has been rotated 90°. The fill of the left shape has become Grey.
7) **a** - One side has been subtracted from each shape.
8) **d** - One side has been subtracted from the shape. The Solid Outline has become Dashed.

9) **b** - The shapes have been swapped, with the fills staying in the same position. The Shaded Fill has been rotated 90°.
10) **d** - The shape has been flipped vertically. The Solid Outline has become Dashed.
11) **e** - The shapes have been swapped with their fills. A Square with a Thick Outline has been added surrounding the figure.
12) **d** - The large shapes have been flipped vertically and have swapped positions. The small shape has remained in the same position in the top shape.
13) **a** - The shapes have been swapped. The outline of the new inner shape has become Solid.
14) **b** - The figure has been rotated 90° anticlockwise. The Black Fill has become White.
15) **e** - The figure has been rotated 45° anticlockwise. The Solid Outline has become Dotted.
16) **c** - The shapes have been swapped with their fills. The Shaded Fill has been rotated 90°.
17) **d** - One shape has become an overlay. The outline of the bottom shape has become Dashed.
18) **a** - The Grey Fill has become White. A Dotted Outline has been added.
19) **e** - The shapes have been rotated 180° individually.
20) **b** - The shape has been flipped vertically. The smaller section has become Grey.

Exercise 19: 3

1) **e** - The figure has been flipped horizontally. The Solid Outline of the outer shape has become Dotted. The Grey Fill has become White.
2) **d** - The Black Fill has become Grey. The shapes have moved up one Line.
3) **b** - The shape has been reduced and has become the bottom shape. A duplicate of the smaller shape has been added as the top shape. The Shaded Fill of the top shape has been rotated 90°.

Answers

11+ Non-verbal Reasoning Year 5-7 Workbook 4

4) **a** - The inner shape has been rotated 90°. A replica of the inner shape has been added to each corner.

5) **e** - The figure has been rotated 90° clockwise. The enclosed Thick Solid Line has become Thin Dashed. The Black Fill has become Grey.

6) **b** - The shape has been reduced and has been duplicated. The Cross-hatched Fill has been split into the two opposite Shaded Fills. The right shape is higher than the left shape.

7) **c** - The figure has been flipped horizontally. The Black and White Fills have been swapped.

8) **b** - A Liquid Fill has been added to the shape. A duplicate of the original shape with a Dashed Outline has been added to the left. The left shape has been rotated 180°.

9) **e** - The shapes have been swapped. The Grey Fill has become Black. The figure has been rotated 90° anticlockwise.

10) **b** - The enclosed Line has been rotated 90° and has become Dotted. The enclosed shapes have remained in the same rotation and have moved clockwise to stay on either side of the Line.

11) **e** - A duplicate of the large shape with a 90° rotation has been added under the original shape. The enclosed shape has been horizontally transposed to outside the figure on the same side.

12) **c** - The figure has been rotated 90° clockwise. The Black Fill has become White. The Solid Outline of the inner shape has become Dotted. The enclosed shape has been rotated 180°.

13) **a** - The White Fill has become Grey. Two sides have been added to the shape. The Thin Outline has become Thick.

14) **e** - The figure has been flipped vertically. The Thin Outline of the bottom shape has become Thick. The shapes have swapped fills.

15) **b** - The Solid Outline has become Dashed. The Arrows have been flipped and moved around the Square.

16) **a** - The figure has been reduced and has become the central enclosed shape. A replica of the original shape with a White Fill has been added surrounding the enclosed shape. A larger replica shape with a Dashed Outline has been added surrounding the new figure.

17) **c** - The White Fill has become Mottled. A smaller replica shape with a 90° anticlockwise rotation has been added as an overlay.

18) **d** - The shape has been enlarged. A replica of the enlarged shape with a Grey Fill has been added as an overlay. The original shape has been rotated 180°.

19) **b** - A replica shape with a 90° rotation and a Dashed Outline has been added as a linkage.

20) **c** - The fill in the middle left square has been horizontally transposed. The fill in the bottom left square has been horizontally transposed. The Cross has been rotated 45°.

Exercise 19: 4

1) **b** - The shape has been rotated 90° anticlockwise. The shape has been split into two and the new bottom shape has been flipped. A White Fill has been added to the new top shape.

2) **c** - The shape has been enlarged and the fill has become White. Small replica shapes with a Grey Fill have been added as overlays to each corner.

3) **d** - The fill of the Square has become Grey. A replica of the figure with a 180° rotation has been added as an overlay and the outline has become Dashed.

4) **a** - The shape has been enlarged and rotated 180°. A replica of the enlarged shape with a Grey Fill has been added as an overlay.

5) **a** - The figure has been rotated 180°. The enclosed shape has been reduced and the fill has been changed to Black. Replicas of the enclosed shape have been put in each corner.

11+ Non-verbal Reasoning
Year 5-7 Workbook 4

Answers

6) **d** - One side has been added to each shape. The fills have been swapped. The outline has become Thick.
7) **c** - The figure has been rotated 90° anticlockwise. The line types have been swapped.
8) **c** - The shape has been enlarged and rotated 180°. A duplicate shape with a half-Grey and half-White Fill has been added behind this shape.
9) **e** - The line types have been swapped. The Black Fills have become White. The Grey Fill has become Black.
10) **a** - The larger shape has been rotated 180°. The inner shape has been rotated 90° anticlockwise. The fills have been swapped.
11) **c** - The figure has been rotated 45°. The Black Fill has become White. The outline of the enclosed shape has become Dashed.
12) **b** - The White and Black Fills have been swapped. The figure has been rotated 90° anticlockwise. The short Line has been vertically transposed. The Square line ending of the short Line has become a Circle.
13) **d** - The Grey Fill has become White. The Black Fill has become White. The Solid Outline has become Dotted. The figure has been rotated 180°.
14) **b** - The fill of the inner shape has become Black and the shape has become the overlay on each corner of the outer shape. The original outer shape has been rotated 45° and the fill has become Grey.
15) **a** - The other half of the large shape has been added on so the large shape has enclosed the two smaller shapes. The figure has been rotated 180°. The fills of the smaller shapes have been swapped.
16) **d** - The Solid Outline has become Dashed. The enclosed shape has been rotated 180° and the fill has become Black. The enclosed shape has been duplicated and a Line has been added in the middle of the large shape, separating the two enclosed shapes.

17) **c** - The figure has been rotated 180°. The Grey Fill has become White. The fills of the outer and inner Squares have been swapped. Dashed and Dotted Lines have been added to the left of the Solid Line.
18) **e** - The shape has been reflected vertically. The White Fill has become Black. A shape with the same number of sides as the number of points on the Star has been added surrounding the Star. A Circle has been added as an overlay on each corner.
19) **a** - The figure has been flipped horizontally. The fills have moved one position inwards. The fill of the small shape has become Black.
20) **b** - A larger replica of the shape with a 90° rotation has been added. The Shaded Fill has been rotated 90°. A replica shape with a Thick Outline has been added around this figure. The original shape has overlaid the bottom of the figure.

Exercise 19: 5

1) **d** - The figure has been flipped horizontally. The opposite Shaded Fill has been added to create a Cross-hatched Fill.
2) **b** - The figure has been reduced and rotated 180°. A duplicate of the smaller shape with a 180° rotation and a White Fill has been added as an overlay.
3) **e** - The Solid Outline has become Dashed. The enclosed shape has been rotated 180°. The left overlay has been rotated 180° and the fill has become Grey. The fill of the right overlay has become White.
4) **b** - The shape has been rotated 90° clockwise and has been reduced to become the top shape. A duplicate of this shape has become the bottom shape. The original shape has been rotated 180° and reduced to become the middle shape. The fill of the middle shape has become Grey.

Answers

11+ Non-verbal Reasoning Year 5-7 Workbook 4

5) **d** - The fills have been swapped. The Shaded Fill has been rotated 90°. The outline has become Thick.
6) **d** - The Arrow has been rotated 180°. The shapes have been swapped.
7) **b** - The outer linked shapes have been removed.
8) **e** - The outline has become Dashed.
9) **e** - The outline has become Thick Solid. The Curved shape has become Straight-edged.
10) **b** - The shape has been rotated 45° anticlockwise.
11) **c** - The shape has been rotated 180°. A replica shape with a Grey Fill has been added as an enclosure. Smaller replicas of the shape with a Black Fill have been added as enclosures at each corner.
12) **c** - One side has been added to the shape. The shape has been reduced and a replica shape with a White Fill has been added. The Shaded Fill has been rotated 90°. The original shape has overlaid the shape with a White Fill.
13) **b** - The line types have been swapped.
14) **d** - Half of the shape has been removed.
15) **c** - The figure has been rotated 90° anticlockwise. A Black Fill has been added to the left of the central shape.
16) **c** - The inner shape has been reduced and the fill has become Grey. The shape has then been overlaid on each corner of the large shape. The fill of the large shape has become White.
17) **a** - The figure has been rotated 180°. The outline has become Thick. The fill of the new left shape has become Black. The new right shape has been rotated 45°.
18) **e** - The inner shape has been rotated 90° anticlockwise. The fills have been swapped.
19) **d** - The figure has been rotated 180°. The smallest shape has changed fill. A Thick Outline that is the same colour as the fill has been added around the shape. The fill of the shape has become White. A small replica shape with a Dashed Outline has been added as the central enclosure.
20) **e** - The figure has been reflected horizontally. The Dashed Outline has become Solid. The original shape with a Dashed Outline has become an overlay.

© 2011 Stephen Curran

PROGRESS CHART

Exercise	Mark	%
17: 1		
17: 2		
17: 3		
17: 4		
17: 5		
18: 1		
18: 2		
18: 3		
18: 4		
18: 5		
19: 1		
19: 2		
19: 3		
19: 4		
19: 5		

Overall Percentage

%

CERTIFICATE OF

ACHIEVEMENT

This certifies

_____

has successfully completed

11+ Non-verbal Reasoning
Year 5–7
WORKBOOK 4

Overall percentage score achieved ☐ %

Comment _____

_____

Signed _____
(teacher/parent/guardian)

Date _____